Qt

The Queeriodic Table

A Celebration of LGBTQ+ Culture

HARRIET DYER

summersdale

THE QUEERIODIC TABLE

An Hachette UK Company
www.hachette.co.uk

Summersdale Publishers Ltd
Part of Octopus Publishing Group Limited
Carmelite House
50 Victoria Embankment
LONDON
EC4Y 0DZ
UK

www.summersdale.com

Printed and bound in the Czech Republic

ISBN: 978-1-78685-752-1

Substantial discounts on bulk quantities of Summersdale books are available to corporations, professional associations and other organisations. For details contact general enquiries: telephone: +44 (0) 1243 771107 or email: enquiries@summersdale.com.

Contents

Introduction

Welcome to *The Queeriodic Table*! Here you will find all the essential elements of queer culture, from history to culture-defining figures; from the hardest struggles to the greatest victories and from the sweetest love story to the campest cult film.

One of the (many) pitfalls of the fact that much of queer history and culture is not taught in schools and is reserved for 'special seasons' on TV and in cinemas, is that people might assume there isn't much to be found. Sure, there are a few queer icons that everyone has heard of and yes, we all know about that one film, but that's about it, right? Queer culture just started in the 1970s and there wasn't anything before that, yes? No! No, no, no! Queer culture is rich and multitextual and extends back to the beginning of known history. Brilliant queer people have been making scientific advances, creating beautiful art, fighting wars and campaigning for peace and civil rights this whole time. The art is out there! The history is out there! The people are out there! It just helps a little to know where to look. Hopefully that's where this book comes in; here are some of the main elements of Western queer culture.

Chapter 1:
Queer History

The first written evidence of the use of the word queer was in 1508, in a poem titled 'The Flyting of Dunbar and Kennedy'. Flyting was a sort of courtly rap battle; a poetic exchange of insults in front of the court; in this case the Scottish court of King James. Dunbar and Kennedy were both real and it appears that this was a genuine exchange that both settled a feud and entertained the court. The use of queer was pejorative but did not obviously refer to sexuality. The line read 'Hey, here comes our own queer clerk' – insulting but rather throwaway in a poem that includes the jibes 'ignorant elf', 'owl irregular' and 'wanfucked foundling'.

Over the years the word queer remained in the English language as an insult, although still a rather nebulous one. The *Dictionary of the Vulgar Tongue*, published in 1785, records several definitions of the word queer. The main entry defines the word as meaning 'roguish' and 'bad'. There are several other entries, including a verb, 'to queer'. According to the dictionary 'to queer the old full bottom' means to puzzle a judge, while a 'queer bluffer' is a crooked innkeeper.

The sad beginning of the word queer as a homophobic slur came in 1894 when the 9th Marquess of Queensbury, architect of more than one tragedy in queer history, used the word as an insult against Lord Rosebery, who he believed had been having a relationship with Queensbury's son Francis. He was writing to his other son, Lord Alfred Douglas, whose lover, Oscar Wilde, he would later send to prison.

This letter was made public during the trial of Oscar Wilde in 1895 and the word queer took on a new, darker life. Usage as a homophobic slur grew; it was used alongside the older, more general definitions at the start of the twentieth century, but by the end of the century the definition had narrowed and it was undeniably targeted hate speech.

Activists started to reclaim the word in the 1980s and 1990s. One of the earliest uses of the word queer by LGBTQ+ groups is the 'Queers Read This' leafleting campaign by LGBT direct-action group Queer Nation. Formed in 1990 by HIV/AIDs activists, Queer Nation campaigned against the appalling levels of violence LGBTQ+ people were facing in their daily lives. The 'Queers Read This' leaflet was distributed at the New York Pride march that year and addressed several subjects, including street violence against LGBT people, the AIDS crisis, queer culture and what it means to be queer. They addressed their use of the word, saying:

'... we've chosen to call ourselves queer. Using "queer" is a way of reminding us how we are perceived by the rest of the world. It's a way of telling ourselves we don't have to be witty and charming people who keep our lives discreet and marginalized in the straight world.'

Queer Nation also weaponised the word queer in several chants, their most famous being 'We're here, we're queer, get used to it!'

The reclamation of the word queer continued. Academics developed 'queer theory' in the 1990s, using it as a lens through which gender and sexuality were studied. Queer theory particularly scrutinised gender roles and how society's enforcement of binary gender roles limited the lives of gay, straight, intersex, trans and cis men and women – so… everyone.

In recent years the usage of queer has widened even further, as the LGBTQ+ umbrella has opened to include more marginalised identities. It's now considered a useful umbrella term that handily encompasses non-conforming genders and sexualities. Some prefer queer to LGBTQ+ because, unlike the initialism, it doesn't name identities, which is seen by some as a way to avoid prioritising some identities over others, or unnecessarily acknowledging the gender/sexuality binary.

Chapter 2:
The Trouble with Sex Is...

… we just don't know what to make of it. Here's a whistle-stop guide to the difference between sex and gender and how society gets these muddled up.

Sex

Sex is a classification system using biological factors, including sex chromosomes, internal genitalia, external genitalia and secondary sex characteristics such as height or hair distribution. Sex is the scientific conclusion drawn from a person's internal and external physical attributes. Or… technically this is the case. Usually all that happens is that a medical professional takes a glance at the crotch area of a baby and assigns them with a sex. In casual conversation, sex and gender tend to be used interchangeably. In fact, sex and gender do not have the same definition. Scientific understanding of sex is constantly evolving, and it is now understood that 'male' and 'female' are not the only two options when it comes to biological sex.

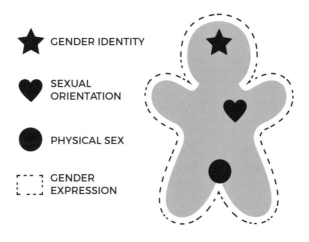

★ GENDER IDENTITY

♥ SEXUAL ORIENTATION

● PHYSICAL SEX

**⌐ ¬ GENDER
└ ┘ EXPRESSION**

A good way to start to get a grip on this is with this scrummy genderbread person. Here you can see that sex is of the body and gender is of the mind. Sex is usually categorised for humans as male, female and intersex. An intersex person is born with sex characteristics that do not wholly belong in either category of male or female.

Gender

Gender is your internal experience of your identity. It's not what your body looks like or acts like, it's how you feel. Gender can be defined by several factors: biological sex and gender expression (see the following page) are the most common. Someone might choose to use one, several or all of these factors to define their gender. Gender identity is rooted in societal ideas about masculinity and femininity, and some gender identities are based on those two points, but there are gender identities that reject masculinity and femininity and stand outside of those. Gender identity is different to your sex, which is based on biology. So a trans man's gender identity is male, but he was assigned female (his 'sex') at birth. Separating gender and sex lets us paint a more accurate picture of the trans experience: a person doesn't change gender, as they were that gender since birth; however, they may choose to alter their sex medically to bring it in line with their gender identity. Gender is not binary – i.e. male or female – but experienced on a spectrum.

Gender Expression

Put simply, gender expression is how you feel in regards to your gender and how you choose to express your gender. Society being as it is, there are informal checklists for this, too. When you dig into it you might be expressing your gender in all sorts of ways, when all you intended to do was simply… exist? Your clothes or your haircut can 'belong' to a gender, your choice of food or drink, your profession or even the toys you play with as a child can be considered gender expression.

Having your gender imposed on you by others can be limiting and disheartening (see Eddie Izzard's excellent line, 'They're not women's clothes, they're my clothes'). But choosing to express your gender however you see fit and flouting the limits of society's imposed gender binary can be very empowering. Some people prefer to use the term 'gender identity', which literally means how an individual would identify their gender (regardless of their assigned gender).

Pronouns

Tiny but mighty, pronouns are some of the building blocks of language. They help us make clear who we're talking about; who said the thing, who did the thing, who is the thing. But the little habits and assumptions need to be challenged just as much as the big ideas. The problem with the English language is that many of its pronouns lock you into the gender binary. Him/her doesn't adequately represent some people's gender expression. Assuming someone's pronouns can cause potential distress for the person who is stuck having to correct an otherwise cool new friend. Most people don't like to inflict pain on others, which can happen when you misgender someone (misgendering is when someone, intentionally or not, assumes someone's gender incorrectly – most commonly through use of incorrect pronouns). But! There are ways around this! One is using new gender-neutral pronouns like zie and zir, replacing he/she and him/her. Another is sticking to an old gender-neutral pronoun, they. (Grammar pedants won't like this, but tough cookies because humans>grammar. Yes, I said it.) The third, and best, option is simply asking someone 'What are your pronouns?' when you meet them.

Chapter 3:
Labels, Labels, Labels

Oh, labels. We humans use them to make things easier and they just don't always work that well. The queer community in particular can have a troubled relationship with labels. Who else has been mislabelled, because someone doesn't understand their identity, with ignorance that ranges from well-meaning to malicious? And yet queer people can be most empowered by labels. It is a strong and affirming act to be able to name yourself, to use a single word that both describes an element of your nature and says 'I am one of many'. Here are some of the most commonly used labels to define gender and sexuality. These definitions may not suit everyone and they may not remain the best words to use in the future; identity and language are both fluid. The important thing is to prioritise a person's feelings on the matter and refer to them in the manner they have requested.

Gay

S
Sexuality

1.

Homosexual and homoromantic. Can refer to people of any gender identity but is most commonly used to refer to someone of male identity who is sexually and romantically attracted to other people who identify as men. One of the reasons in favour of using the word queer as an umbrella term over gay is that gay does prioritise the male sexual experience. The word potentially referred to same-gender-loving people as far back as the late nineteenth century, although recorded references start to pop up around the early to mid-twentieth century.

Lesbian

S
Sexuality

2.

Someone who identifies as a woman who is sexually and romantically attracted to other people who identify as women. For most of history 'lesbian' simply referred to anyone or anything that came from the Isle of Lesbos in the Aegean Sea. It came to mean a woman who is attracted to other women thanks to the cultural effect of the famous poet Sappho (p.39), who lived on the Isle of Lesbos in the late seventh to early sixth centuries BC and wrote about her love for women. Lesbian was in use as a description of same-gender love as early as the late nineteenth century; 'sapphist', also from Sappho, was popular at the same time.

Homosexual

3.

S
Sexuality

A sexual preference for people of the same gender identity. Like heterosexual, this is one that has come to mean an all-round preference for people of the same gender, rather than just sexy feelings. This one is a bit clinical for everyday use and chimes especially uncomfortably against the word straight (which would be heterosexual, if one were using words with parity). When you use it in reference to people it can sound like you're categorising them, so it's often better to use 'gay' or 'lesbian' where those words apply. Of course, as with all terms in this book, personal preference rules all! If a person you're talking to prefers 'homosexual' to any other term, then use that one!

Heterosexual

S
Sexuality

4.

A sexual preference exclusively for people of a different gender. Commonly used as an umbrella term for a preference for romantic as well as sexual relationships with people of a different gender. Slang includes 'straight'; a term which developed from mid-twentieth-century gay slang. It originally referred to queer people who would 'go straight', as in live on the 'straight and narrow'. This would mean that they would choose to live in the closet. Straight is now commonly used to refer to people who have identified as heterosexual all their lives.

Bisexual

5.

S
Sexuality

Sexual attraction towards people of the same gender as well as people of other genders. Often used as an umbrella term to include biromanticism (a person who feels romantic attraction to people of the same and other genders). It isn't always the case that a person will be both biromantic and bisexual; some people have sexual urges towards people of any gender but prefer only to be in romantic relationships with a person of a particular gender. Some people see the 'bi' in bisexual as assuming that gender is binary and includes only two genders, which erases the experience of people who identify as genderqueer or non-binary.

Pansexual

6.

S
Sexuality

A person who has sexual urges towards and is sexually attracted to people of any gender. This can encompass romantic feelings too, although that can be separately covered under the term 'panromantic'. At first glance the definition of pansexual is the same as that of bisexual. However, the use of the word 'pan' is intended to open up the definition past the binary 'attracted to men and women' of bisexual and include attraction to people who appear anywhere on the gender spectrum. Not everyone agrees that the bisexual identity has those limitations on gender identity: ultimately personal choice is the decision-maker when it comes to the language you choose to identify yourself.

Asexual

S
Sexuality

7.

Someone who does not usually feel sexual attraction or a sexual urge towards other people. Asexuality works on a spectrum, like sexuality; some people who consider themselves to be asexual never feel sexual attraction or urges; others do on occasion. Some are averse to any sexual touch or interaction, others engage in it on occasion to please their partners or themselves. An asexual identity doesn't have to stem from a revulsion against sex; some asexual identities simply don't find sex interesting, fulfilling or important.

Transgender

8.

G
Gender

Someone whose true gender identity is different to the gender they were assigned at birth based on their sex. This can mean their gender is 'binary'; they were assigned male/female at birth and identify as female/male. Or they might identify as genderfluid or non-binary and their body does not fully represent their gender identity. As gender is an internal experience and not a person's sex characteristics, someone might identify as transgender and have only partial or no surgery to alter their sex characteristics. A commonly used abbreviation for transgender is 'trans'.

Cisgender

9.

G
Gender

A cisgender person is one whose assigned-at-birth gender matches their gender identity. Using this term avoids establishing a default or 'normal' and acknowledges that everyone has a relationship between their birth gender and gender identification. A commonly used abbreviation for cisgender is 'cis'.

Agender

G
Gender

10.

Someone who does not identify as any particular gender; genderless. Other terms that have a similar meaning to agender include gender-neutral or neutrois. A person who identifies as agender does not identify with any gender identity on the gender spectrum, including male and female. They may choose to use gender-neutral pronouns such as zie or zir – the eternal truth holds here: it is always better to ask someone's preferred pronouns and use those.

Genderfluid

11.

G
Gender

A person whose gender is not fixed, or is able or likely to change. This term indicates that a person's gender identity moves within the spectrum it exists on. The fluidity of an identity can be felt at any time or in response to certain circumstances. The person's identity can be weighted more to one area of the spectrum or can fluctuate evenly between different identities.

Gender-neutral

12.

G
Gender

1. An identification where a person does not identify as one gender more than any other gender, see also agender (p.23). Can be different to androgyny, which engages with the gender spectrum to produce an effect that incorporates two or more genders.

2. Something which is not about or intended for one gender over another. Gender-neutrality can be useful in all sorts of ways. One example is its increasing usage in job titles – for example, fire officer instead of firewoman or fireman (it's unlikely the gender of the person putting out your fire will matter in the heat of the moment). Another is products for children such as clothes or toys; campaigners have argued against the segregation of toys by gender, saying that it's up to the child to decide and that some children might get gender-policed (judged, made the subject of comments or attacked based on how they are expressing their gender) just because they don't play with the 'right' toy.

Chapter 4:
Key Events

Here are a few timelines charting different events in queer history. If you are a bit of a history buff and want to know everything that the history books haven't told you, there is more to be found in the further reading section. The timelines that follow are a good way to get started, as you might learn about a few historical figures or historical practices that you hadn't heard of. For example, you may be pleasantly surprised to learn that pirates had a long and storied history of same-sex marriage that included death benefits for bereaved partners (pirates were surprisingly bureaucratic). These marriages were often open to including other lovers (pirates, not so surprisingly, loved the booty). And did you know that one of Rome's most beloved and militaristic emperors was openly gay – although they did not use that terminology – and that citizens trying to curry favour or apologise for wrong doings would often send along their handsome sons to try to add a little charm? Read on, and you may find a few surprises.

Across All of Time and Space
A history of queerness in world culture

371 BC

The Sacred Band of Thebes, an elite force of the Theban army consisting of 150 pairs of male lovers, defeats the powerful Spartan army at the Battle of Leuctra.

Eighth century BC

Rock art in Zimbabwe depicts gay sex, including a threesome.

*c.*1000 BC

Native Americans are flourishing in North America. Tribes including the Ojibwe, Navajo and Cheyenne have words in their language for those of their population who identify as other than their birth sex: the Ojibwe *niizh manidoowag*, the Navajo *Nádleehí* and the Cheyenne *Hemaneh*.

*c.*400 BC

The *Kama Sutra* contains a chapter dedicated to homosexual sex.

Second century BC

Khnumhotep and Niankhkhnum, two high-level ancient Egyptian servants, are buried together. One painting depicts them standing nose-to-nose while another portrays Khnumhotep standing with Niankhkhnum in the position usually reserved for a wife.

57 BC

Catullus writes homoerotic poetry to a male lover.

*c.*1100

The medieval Arabic word for 'lesbian' is *sihaqa. The Encyclopedia of Pleasure* stated that lesbianism was caused by too much heat in the labia; the prescribed cure was for the 'sufferer' to rub their genitals against another woman's genitals.

AD 98

Roman emperor Trajan takes the throne. He is one of Rome's most beloved emperors and openly gay.

1593

Christopher Marlowe writes *Edward II*, a historical play about England's purportedly gay King Edward II and his lover Piers Gaveston. One of its passages lists famous historical and fictional lovers, including Alexander the Great and Hephaestion, Achilles and Patroclus and Socrates and Alcibiades.

1632

Queen Christina comes to the throne of Sweden. She was noted in her time for her masculine dress and behaviour. She has been romantically connected to both men and women; contemporary accounts report her introducing lady-in-waiting Ebba Sparre as her bedfellow.

1726

Mother Clap's Molly House in London is raided. Run by Margaret Clap, the house was a sort of inn or tavern where gay men were welcome to rent a bed to sleep with their lovers. Mother Clap's was infamous at the time due to the raid but many others of its like existed around the city.

1930

Lili Elbe is one of the first people in the world to undergo sex reassignment surgery – now referred to as gender confirmation surgery – in Germany.

1948

Alfred Kinsey, biologist and sexologist, publishes the Kinsey scale, which portrays sexual attraction on a scale. This revolutionised first scientific and then popular thinking on sexuality: sexual attraction had previously been thought to be fixed and binary – either heterosexual or homosexual.

1880s

The Hundred Guineas Club in London opens. The entrance fee was, not surprisingly, one hundred guineas (around $10,000 today – an exclusive crowd) and it was a place where well-off gay men could safely bring their lovers or pick up prostitutes.

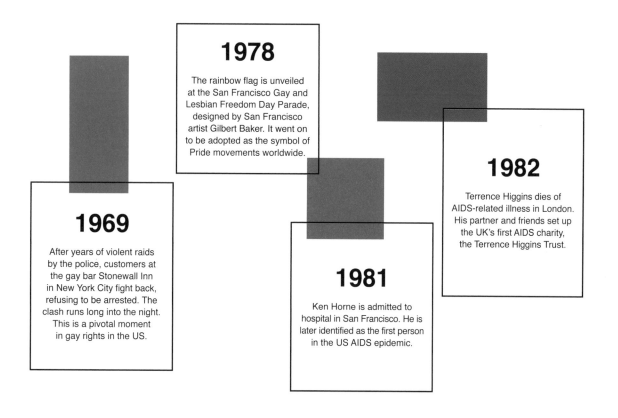

1978

The rainbow flag is unveiled at the San Francisco Gay and Lesbian Freedom Day Parade, designed by San Francisco artist Gilbert Baker. It went on to be adopted as the symbol of Pride movements worldwide.

1982

Terrence Higgins dies of AIDS-related illness in London. His partner and friends set up the UK's first AIDS charity, the Terrence Higgins Trust.

1969

After years of violent raids by the police, customers at the gay bar Stonewall Inn in New York City fight back, refusing to be arrested. The clash runs long into the night. This is a pivotal moment in gay rights in the US.

1981

Ken Horne is admitted to hospital in San Francisco. He is later identified as the first person in the US AIDS epidemic.

Love in the Time of Intolerance
Queer unions in world history

27 BC

The first recorded same-sex marriage takes place in the Roman Empire, under the reign of Augustus.

Fifth century BC

Motsoalle, erotic friendships between Basotho women in the African country of Lesotho, are recorded. These took place alongside heterosexual marriages. There were feasts celebrating *motsoalle* relationships, with the last being held in 1980 (when they were stopped under colonial rule; colonising forces are held responsible in many societies for introducing homophobic laws worldwide).

630 BC

Men in Cretan society form lifelong romantic relationships with other men that are recognised by society. The origins of the relationships were paederastic, often starting when the younger man was in his teens with the elder acting as a mentor as well as a lover.

c. Fourth century BC

The *Ramayana* speaks of the Hijra, people of a third gender, to whom Prince Rama granted the ability to bless couples with fertility on the occasion of their marriage. The Hijra appear in other ancient texts with the same ability. They are today legally recognised by some South Asian countries as being of a third gender.

Tenth century

The *Encyclopedia of Pleasure*, an early Arabic erotic work by Ali ibn Nasr al-Katib, tells of the love between a Muslim woman, Hind Bint al-Khuss al-Iyadiyyah, and a Christian woman, Hind Bint al-Nu`man, who spent their lives together.

AD 1061

Two men, Pedro Diaz and Muño Vandilaz, are married by a Catholic priest in Galicia, Spain.

*c.*1400

Affrèrement contracts are drawn up in France during the late medieval period. They were domestic contracts built around cohabitation in which two men swear to share 'one bread, one wine and one purse'.

1600s

Marriage between male pirates is common. It was called matelotage, after the French word for sailor, *matelot*. Matelot partners shared their loot from their voyages and ships even paid a deceased sailor's portion to their surviving partner. The word is also where the term 'matey' originated!

1880s

In New England, USA the term 'Boston Marriage' is used to refer to two women who live together independent of financial support from a man. These unions were sometimes romantic in nature.

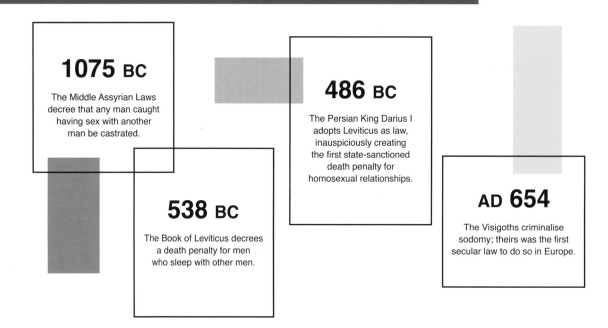

1075 BC

The Middle Assyrian Laws decree that any man caught having sex with another man be castrated.

538 BC

The Book of Leviticus decrees a death penalty for men who sleep with other men.

486 BC

The Persian King Darius I adopts Leviticus as law, inauspiciously creating the first state-sanctioned death penalty for homosexual relationships.

AD 654

The Visigoths criminalise sodomy; theirs was the first secular law to do so in Europe.

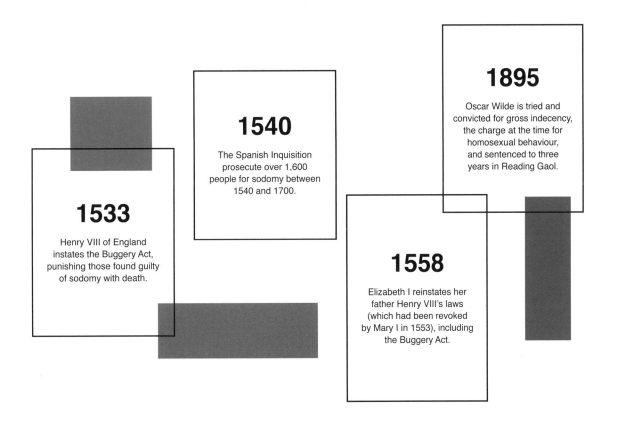

1533

Henry VIII of England instates the Buggery Act, punishing those found guilty of sodomy with death.

1540

The Spanish Inquisition prosecute over 1,600 people for sodomy between 1540 and 1700.

1558

Elizabeth I reinstates her father Henry VIII's laws (which had been revoked by Mary I in 1553), including the Buggery Act.

1895

Oscar Wilde is tried and convicted for gross indecency, the charge at the time for homosexual behaviour, and sentenced to three years in Reading Gaol.

1967

The Sexual Offences Act decriminalises homosexual activity between two men over the age of 21 in the UK.

2000

Lesbian, gay and bisexual people are no longer banned from serving in the military in the UK.

2013

The UK legalises same-sex marriage.

1988

Section 28 of the Local Government Act is introduced in the UK under Prime Minister Margaret Thatcher. It prohibits any portrayal of homosexuality as acceptable in schools.

2010

The US policy of 'Don't Ask Don't Tell' for LGB people serving in the military is lifted.

2018

Australia legalises same-sex marriage.

2015

The USA legalises same-sex marriage across all states.

Countries that now perform same-sex marriage include Argentina, Australia, Austria, Belgium, Brazil, Canada, Colombia, Costa Rica, Denmark, Finland, France, Germany, Iceland, Ireland, Luxembourg, Malta, Mexico, Netherlands, New Zealand, Norway, Portugal, South Africa, Spain, Sweden, Taiwan, United Kingdom, United States, Uruguay.

Countries that still outlaw homosexuality include Afghanistan, Bangladesh, Cameroon, Indonesia, Iran, Jamaica, Mauritania, Nigeria, Pakistan, Qatar, Saudi Arabia, Sierra Leone, Singapore, UAE, Yemen.

Chapter 5:
Game Changers

Queer game changers come in all shapes and sizes, from all corners of history. Some changed the whole world, others influenced public perceptions about queer people through their lives and their work. Some were skilled mathematicians, others artists. There are some names you may know well, others who have faded a little from the limelight, or were never given the chance they deserved. All were brave, brilliant and utterly deserving of attention. Now is the time to turn the spotlight back on to them and celebrate everything they have done for us.

Sappho

630–570 BC

> **I DECLARE THAT LATER ON, EVEN IN AN AGE UNLIKE OUR OWN, SOMEONE WILL REMEMBER WHO WE ARE.**

13.

Not much is known of Sappho's life: she was born into a wealthy family on Lesbos in 630 BC and was probably married. Even her poetry, supposed to once number around 10,000 lines, only survives in fragments, with just one complete poem. However, she was astonishingly successful in her lifetime and her poetry was influential for nearly a thousand years after her death. Plato referred to her as the 'tenth muse' and she was considered one of the nine 'canonical lyric poets of Ancient Greece' – meaning she was an essential part of any comprehensive Ancient Greek literary education. The subjects of her poetry were many but she is most famous for her erotic writing about women. Poems include 'Fragment One', where Sappho (named in the text) implores the goddess Aphrodite to induce her female love to return her affection, and 'Fragment Thirty-one', which describes yearning for a girl. The words 'sapphic' and 'lesbian' derive respectively from her name and her place of birth. Her cultural and historic standing has led to her adoption as a lesbian – and feminist – icon.

14.

Edward Carpenter

1844–1929

Edward Carpenter was a Victorian scholar and philosopher who campaigned for social causes including workers' rights and gay rights. Perhaps his best-remembered works are the socialist marching song 'England, Arise!' and his essay 'Civilisation: Its Cause and Cure'. His four-book prose poem *Towards Democracy* explores his creeds and contains overt explorations of his gay passions and desires. Carpenter was very radical for his time; he not only published poems and essays exploring and advocating for gay rights but lived openly with the love of his life, George Merrill, for nearly thirty years. The couple even inspired E. M. Forster to write *Maurice* (p.100) after Forster visited the pair (rather sweetly, the reserved Forster recorded that the exact moment he conceived of *Maurice* was when Merrill touched Forster's bottom). Carpenter was hugely influential; he numbered among his correspondents Walt Whitman, D. H. Lawrence, John Ruskin, Isadora Duncan and Mahatma Gandhi. During World War One he received many letters from gay servicemen, including Siegfried Sassoon, thanking him for helping them come to terms with their sexuality.

> ❝ REAL LOVE IS ONLY POSSIBLE IN THE FREEDOM OF SOCIETY; AND FREEDOM IS ONLY POSSIBLE WHEN LOVE IS A REALITY. ❞

Oscar Wilde

1854–1900

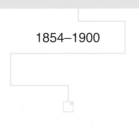

TO DENY ONE'S OWN EXPERIENCES IS TO PUT A LIE INTO THE LIPS OF ONE'S OWN LIFE. IT IS NO LESS THAN A DENIAL OF THE SOUL.

15.

Gc
Game Changers

Although he never identified as gay, Oscar Wilde has been one of the most influential queer figures in history. His glamorous rise and dramatic fall influenced queer culture in the UK for years to come. His famous trial, in which he was charged with sodomy and gross indecency, and subsequent imprisonment, sent a ripple of fear through queer communities in the UK. While there had been other arrests and prosecutions of queer people in the era, the downfall of one of the UK's most famous celebrities was galling. His novel *The Picture of Dorian Gray* was used on the stand against him and although most of its queer content is subtext, it is still one of the most culturally impactful queer texts today. Although his downfall is a lasting testament to the treatment of queer people throughout history, it is important also to look to his triumphs. Who in the world has ever been wittier than Oscar Wilde? Who has spanned literary achievement so triumphantly, from a screwball social satirical play (*The Importance of Being Earnest*) to a stunning tragic play (*Salome*); from a biting, beautiful novel (*The Picture of Dorian Gray*) to childhood classic short stories like *The Selfish Giant*?

16.

Gc
Game Changers

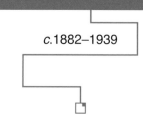

Ma Rainey

*c.*1882–1939

Ma Rainey was known as Mother of the Blues and was one of the first women to find commercial success singing the blues. She was well-known and toured the country extensively, as well as recording nearly a hundred records, including several singles with Louis Armstrong. Rainey's songs, which she wrote herself, include references to loving men and women. Her most explicitly queer song, 'Prove It On Me', was supposedly written after Rainey was arrested at an orgy with her backing singers and dancers, and refers to a woman that Rainey intends to 'follow wherever she goes'. She mentored Bessie Smith, one of the most influential early blues singers who herself had affairs with both men and women in her lifetime. As the popularity of the blues gave way to swing in the 1930s Rainey retired from performing live and ran a theatre, until she died prematurely of a heart attack in her fifties.

Claude Cahun

1894–1954

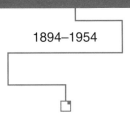

❝ UNDER THIS MASK, ANOTHER MASK. I WILL NEVER BE FINISHED REMOVING ALL THESE FACES. ❞

17.

Gc
Game Changers

Claude Cahun was a French-Jewish woman who experimented heavily with self-portrait, using her art to examine gender presentation and traditional gender roles in society; her mesmerising work, 'Self-Portrait, 1928', portrays her standing in front of a mirror but staring at a camera, with a shaved head and dressed in a masculine checked jacket. She is sometimes classed as a surrealist artist, having developed a surrealist edge after befriending André Breton, the founding father of the movement. She fell in love at a young age with her stepsister Marcel Moore and the pair were inseparable for the rest of their lives. In 1937 they moved to Jersey in the Channel Islands. When, in 1940, Nazi Germany occupied Jersey the pair were forced to present themselves as sisters. With immense courage, they both started distributing anti-Nazi propaganda, sometimes stealing into parties full of German officers and slipping notes into their jacket pockets. In 1944 their resistance actions were discovered and they were sentenced to death, and the Nazis destroyed much of Claude's art. The pair were saved by the Liberation of Jersey in 1945 and they continued to live together as lovers on Jersey until Cahun's death in 1954.

Gc
Game Changers

18.

Marlene Dietrich rose to fame in the 1920s Berlin cabaret scene, an era known for its sexual freedom and gender expression. Although married, she was known as a 'garconne'; a woman who sexually pursued whomever she liked regardless of their gender. Her early German film roles reflected these origins; she was often cast in the role of a dangerous woman or femme fatale who performed in a club. She shot *Der Blaue Engel* (*The Blue Angel*) in 1929 with director Josef von Sternberg, which launched her career in Hollywood. She somewhat softened her image for the more conservative American audiences but still maintained her androgynous glamour; watch the 1930 film *Morocco* to see her slinking around a nightclub in a tuxedo and kissing a woman (one of the earliest lesbian kisses in Hollywood). Although she was never truly 'out' to the public, she was known in Hollywood for her affairs with both men and women (reportedly referring to the lesbian and bisexual women in Hollywood as 'the sewing circle'). She numbered among her lovers Gary Cooper, John Wayne, Erich Maria Remarque, Mercedes de Acosta and Edith Piaf.

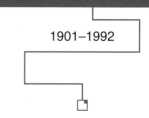

Marlene Dietrich

1901–1992

❝ COURAGE AND GRACE IS A FORMIDABLE MIXTURE. ❞

Quentin Crisp

1908–1999

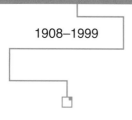

> **I BECAME A PROTOTYPE OF THE EFFEMINATE MAN, BECAUSE I WAS CONSPICUOUSLY EFFEMINATE. BUT CAMP IS NOT SOMETHING I DO, IT'S SOMETHING I AM.**

19.

Gc
Game Changers

Of his sexuality, author, flamboyant personality and gay icon Quentin Crisp said, 'I was never in [the closet]!' Crisp lived a full and wild life in London, often wearing make-up and scraping a living modelling for artists, before he found fame in 1968 with his memoir *The Naked Civil Servant*. The public discovered his acerbic wit and were fascinated by his account of living an openly gay life in wartime and post-war Britain. Soon he became an unabashedly eccentric raconteur, filling theatres with audiences desperate to hear the stories of his life. In his seventies, Crisp fulfilled a lifetime dream and moved to Manhattan's East Village. Here he enjoyed perhaps his most prosperous years: he continued to fill theatres and also took up acting, taking small parts in TV and on film, even appearing as Elizabeth I in a 1992 adaptation of Virginia Woolf's queer text *Orlando* (see p.103).

20.

Gc
Game Changers

Bayard Rustin

1912–1987

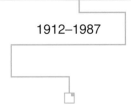

Bayard Rustin worked tirelessly throughout his life for the betterment of humanity, specifically campaigning to improve civil rights and gay rights in America. Rustin worked with leaders of the American civil rights movement such as A. Philip Randolph and Martin Luther King to protest the working and living conditions of black Americans. His work with Randolph on the March on Washington Movement exerted enough pressure on President Roosevelt that the president agreed to desegregate the military, despite having been previously reluctant to do so. Rustin is somewhat forgotten as a civil rights leader; as an out gay man who had previously belonged to the Communist Party, he attracted vicious attacks from the opposition and preferred to work behind the scenes as an advisor, slipping from popular memory in the years after his death. Later in life Rustin turned his hand to campaigning for gay rights, testifying for New York's Gay Rights Bill. Rustin even gave impassioned speeches on LGBT rights at universities, something he had shied away from earlier in his career.

❝ YOU HAVE TO JOIN EVERY OTHER MOVEMENT FOR THE FREEDOM OF PEOPLE. ❞

Alan Turing

1912–1954

WE CAN ONLY SEE A SHORT DISTANCE AHEAD, BUT WE CAN SEE PLENTY THERE THAT NEEDS TO BE DONE.

21.

Gc
Game Changers

Had Alan Turing achieved only a fraction of his life's works, then his life would still be astonishing. Gifted in mathematics, Turing published several significant computing papers as a student in his early twenties. He advanced the thinking on how computers could work and where their limitations lay; machines that follow the algorithms he set out are now called Turing Machines. A few years later, at the start of World War Two, Turing reported to Bletchley Park, where he would help to develop a system to decrypt encoded German messages from the 'unbreakable' Enigma machine, containing vital information about the Axis powers' movements. After the war Turing continued to make significant mathematical and mathematical biology breakthroughs; his work on artificial intelligence defines how we think of AI today (the test to determine whether a computer is 'thinking' is called the Turing Test). It is safe to say that the world would not be as it is today without Alan Turing. Sadly, following a burglary at his house where the police learned he had been in a relationship with a man, Turing was arrested and convicted for 'gross indecency'. He was chemically castrated and took his own life a few years after.

Gc
Game Changers

22.

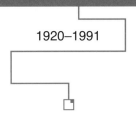

Tom of Finland

1920–1991

Tom of Finland was the artistic pseudonym of Finnish artist Touko Laaksonen. His hyper-butch erotic illustrations of gay men have a cult status in the mainstream art world and he has left a lasting legacy in homoerotic queer art. His illustrated men are characterised by bulging muscles, often wearing fetishised uniforms or labourer's gear. He started his career in the 1950s by submitting his illustrations to homoerotic magazines masquerading as fitness magazines, such as *Physique Pictorial*. As US pornographic censorship faded, Laaksonen was able to publish more explicit work and more openly, including releasing comics and volumes of books. Laaksonen's portrayals of happy, butch, muscular men contradicted the homophobic assumptions of the time that gay men were weak and unhappy and created a place for a positive portrayal of gay sexuality. In his lifetime Laaksonen discussed the hope that his art would one day be seen in even a 'small side room' of a museum such as the Louvre; MOMA now possess several Tom of Finland pieces in their permanent collection.

> **" I WANTED MY DRAWINGS TO... SHOW GAY MEN BEING HAPPY AND POSITIVE ABOUT WHO THEY WERE. "**

Christine Jorgensen

1926–1989

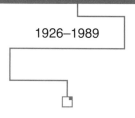

" **EVERYONE IS BOTH SEXES IN VARYING DEGREES. I AM MORE OF A WOMAN THAN A MAN.** "

23.

Christine Jorgensen was the first American recipient of gender confirmation surgery and the first person in the world to be given a course of hormones as part of their treatment. At the time, in 1952, the only doctor prepared to give her the treatment was in Denmark and so she travelled there, obscuring the reason for her visit. On her return she found the news of the true reason for her trip had leaked and she was greeted by a horde of press. 'Ex-GI becomes blonde beauty' screamed headlines. Faced with a nationwide obsession with her body, Jorgensen chose to use the opportunity to spread knowledge about transgender lives. She gave interviews to national papers and embarked on lecture tours, responding to intrusive questions about her body and her sex life with notable grace. For a while she was something of a celebrity; she received offers of acting jobs from Hollywood, was invited to star-studded parties and embarked on a nightclub career that ended with her dressed as Wonder Woman. Of her time in the spotlight, Jorgensen said, 'We didn't start the sexual revolution but I think we gave it a good kick in the pants!'

Harvey Milk

1930–1978

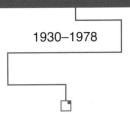

Gc
Game Changers

Harvey Milk is known as the first openly gay person to hold an elected position in America. This isn't quite accurate – Kathy Kozachenko was elected to a seat on the Ann Arbor City Council in 1974, four years before Milk's term of service, and Elaine Noble was elected to the Massachusetts House of Representatives in 1975. He is, however, one of the best-known early LGBTQ+ political pioneers in the USA. Milk was elected to the San Francisco Board of Supervisors in November 1977, serving from 1978. During his time on the board he threw his weight and political prowess behind several historically important LGBTQ+ causes. He sponsored a bill that outlawed discrimination based on sexual orientation; the bill was passed and was considered one of the strongest bits of pro-LGBTQ+ legislation in the nation.

Milk also successfully campaigned against Prop 6, a proposed Californian law which would have banned any out LGBTQ+ people from working in public schools. Milk's campaign against Prop 6 garnered influential political support, including from former President Jimmy Carter and former governor of California Ronald Reagan. Prop 6 was overwhelmingly rejected in early November 1978. Milk's political star was on the rise when, on 27 November 1978, a disgruntled former employee of the Board of Supervisors broke in to City Hall and shot the mayor of San Francisco and Harvey Milk. It is a tragedy that Harvey Milk was killed, and that he never had the opportunity to build on the great works he had already achieved. The public outcry over his death and the short sentence of his killer shook the American political system and arguably helped pave the way for other out elected officials such as Gerry Studds and Barney Franks to serve.

HOPE WILL NEVER BE SILENT.

25.

Gc
Game Changers

Ann Bannon's 'Beebo Brinker' novels follow the lives of young lesbian women in the 1950s and contain one of literature's greatest butch characters, Beebo Brinker. Written in the late 1950s and early 1960s and starting with *Odd Girl Out*, they follow a group of sorority girlfriends as they explore their sexuality and move to New York City. There they meet Beebo, who is handsome, young and 'swashbuckling' and who refuses to wear women's clothing. Bannon was unhappily married to a man at the time of writing her novels. For many years she was unaware of the impact her novels had had on lesbian literature and the lesbian pulp fiction genre. Her legacy developed during the 1970s and 1980s as the LGBTQ+ rights movement grew and many women recalled her novels as their first glimpse of queer characters with complex lives and (relatively) happy endings. Her books are still in print today.

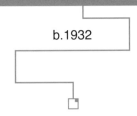

Ann Bannon

b.1932

❝ WE DID ACHIEVE SOMETHING. WE BUILT A BRIDGE TO ISOLATED, FRIGHTENED WOMEN AND TOLD THEM THEY WERE NOT ALONE. ❞

Audre Lorde

1934–1992

> **I HAVE COME TO BELIEVE THAT CARING FOR MYSELF IS NOT SELF-INDULGENT. CARING FOR MYSELF IS AN ACT OF SURVIVAL.**

Audre Lorde's poem 'Spring' was published in *Seventeen* magazine when she was 15. It was her first published piece and the start of a starred poetry career. Poetry was her first forum for publicly exploring the issues that she would confront throughout her multi-avenued career. While her reputation as a poet was growing, Lorde was also campaigning against the Vietnam War and attending civil rights and feminist rallies. She styled herself a 'black lesbian mother warrior poet', refusing to allow that any one politicised identity should take precedence over the other. Lorde scrutinised the predominantly white second-wave feminist movement and her poems, essays and speeches were instrumental in creating a space in the movement for black feminists. Her book *Sister Outsider*, for which she is perhaps best known, is a searing collection of essays and poems that explore what it means to be a black lesbian woman in the USA. Lorde survived cancer twice in her forties and she chronicled her journey in *The Cancer Journals*, adding memoirist to her list of talents. Sadly, a year after she was appointed Poet Laureate of New York, Audre Lorde lost her battle with breast cancer.

Gc

27.

Game Changers

April Ashley

April Ashley underwent gender confirmation surgery in 1960, at a time when such procedures were still relatively unknown. In fact, the surgeon who operated on her had only completed seven surgeries before hers. After her surgery in Casablanca, Ashley returned to Britain and begun a successful modelling career. She was *Vogue's* favourite lingerie model for a while, photographed by David Bailey. She even secured a small walk-on part in the Bing Crosby film *The Road to Hong Kong*. Unfortunately, only six months in to her success a former friend sold Ashley's story to newspaper the *Sunday People* (for £5) and her career broke down under the scrutiny of the tabloids. She, and trans rights, were dealt a further blow when she was subjected to gender 'tests' by her estranged husband, even though he had known about Ashley's background when they married, simply because he wanted to avoid paying a divorce settlement. The judge ruled that she was legally a man and that her marriage was null, setting a precedent for the UK's legal definition of gender to be a person's birth sex that would last until the 2004 Gender Recognition Act. She continued to campaign for legal reform throughout her life and in 2012 she was awarded an OBE for services to transgender equality.

b.1935

" IT WAS AS THOUGH MY BRAIN WAS IN TUNE WITH THE REST OF MY BODY FOR THE FIRST TIME IN MY LIFE. "

Wendy Carlos

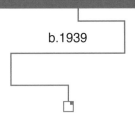

b.1939

" AS HUMAN BEINGS WE DO CHANGE, GROW, ADAPT, PERHAPS EVEN LEARN AND BECOME WISER. "

28.

Gc
Game Changers

Wendy Carlos is an award-winning electronic artist and film composer. Her three film scores are among the most iconic electronic scores in history: *A Clockwork Orange*, *The Shining* and *Tron*. Her first album, *Switched-On Bach*, an electronic take on Bach's music which she released under her birth name, Walter Carlos, was the first classical album ever to go platinum. Released in 1968, it was an instant hit. However, since Carlos's success coincided with the start of her hormone treatment, it was a difficult time for her to be thrust into the public eye. For public appearances such as *The Dick Cavett Show* or conducting the St Louis Symphony Orchestra she presented as a man, wearing fake facial hair and drawing in her eyebrows. In 1971, while working on Stanley Kubrick's *A Clockwork Orange*, she changed her name to Wendy, although she still released albums under the name Walter. She publicly acknowledged her transition in 1979 in an interview to *Playboy* magazine. Her career continued to grow, as she reunited with Kubrick for *The Shining* and then worked with Disney on *Tron*, as well as releasing an album with 'Weird Al' Yankovic. Of the public reaction to her transition Carlos commented, 'the public have turned out to be amazingly tolerant or… indifferent'. She is one of the most famous trans composers and influential electronic composers living today.

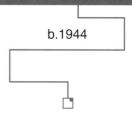

Gc

29.
Game Changers

Rita Mae Brown's debut novel *Rubyfruit Jungle* is her most enduring; an ebullient coming-of-age story that describes a girl's exploration of her own sexuality. The tale is semi-autobiographical and was so successful that the small feminist press that was publishing it couldn't keep up with the print demands. Brown was open about her sexuality at all times and has commented that so few others were willing to be open that she felt like the only 'lesbian in America'. She has been politically active all her life and has campaigned on the part of civil rights, gay rights and feminism. She was thrown out of the National Organisation for Women for campaigning for lesbian rights to be on their agenda, something Betty Friedan, one of the founding members of the organisation, later apologised for. Brown resists the labels of 'gay' and 'straight', commenting that those are labels used by the oppressors and that queer people who use them put themselves in boxes.

Rita Mae Brown

b.1944

❝ BECAUSE NOBODY HAD EVER SAID THESE THINGS AND USED THEIR REAL NAME, I SUDDENLY BECAME THE ONLY LESBIAN IN AMERICA. ❞

Divine

1945–1988

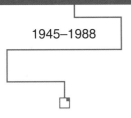

❝ I'M A HAPPY PERSON DOING WHAT I WANT TO DO AND I'M NOT HURTING ANYBODY. ❞

30.

Divine was the stage name and drag persona of actor and musician Harris Glenn Milstead. He became interested in counter culture in his early twenties, where he met filmmaker John Waters. The two began collaborating and Milstead appeared, as Divine, in many of Waters' early films. Now cult classics, the films were exercises in making the most gloriously trashy movies possible; in perhaps his most notorious scene, in *Pink Flamingos* Divine eats dog faeces on camera. He also originated the role Edna Turnblad in Waters' most mainstream hit, *Hairspray*. Milstead himself, as Divine, was also starting to experience mainstream success. His musical career was taking off, with hits such as 'I'm So Beautiful' being played in discos around the world. Divine even appeared on UK family chart show *Top of the Pops* with his single 'You Think You're a Man'. He counted many celebrities among his fans and was the subject for artists such as David Hockney and personal friend Andy Warhol. Sadly, only a few weeks after *Hairspray* was released and on the day he was supposed to film a guest appearance for American sitcom *All My Children*, Milstead died of an enlarged heart. Although mainstream success eluded him, he remains a cult queer icon.

Gc

31.

Game Changers

Marsha P. Johnson is alleged to have 'thrown the first brick' at the Stonewall Inn uprising, when the LGBT clientele at Stonewall Inn fought back against the humiliating raids conducted by the New York police department. Accounts of that night, including her own, differ, but what is clear is that Johnson was among those that fought the hardest that night. In the years that followed she would continue to campaign tirelessly for the rights of LGBTQ+ people, even while she herself battled with homelessness and mental illness. She participated in and helped to organise the Gay Liberation Front marches in New York, which would later become Pride. With Sylvia Rivera (p.61) she would set up STAR, Street Transvestite Action Revolutionaries, a charity and shelter for homeless transgender teens. Later she campaigned for better access to medicine for AIDS patients. In her lifetime Johnson used female pronouns and referred to herself variously as a drag queen, gay man and transvestite; she would say (sometimes in court) that the 'P' in her name stood for 'pay it no mind', referring to her gender. In 1992 she died in suspicious circumstances, and although the authorities initially labelled it suicide, activist Mariah Lopez managed to get her case reopened in 2012.

Marsha P. Johnson

1945–1992

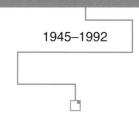

" DARLING, I WANT MY GAY RIGHTS NOW! "

Freddie Mercury

1946–1991

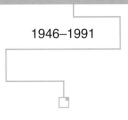 **I WON'T BE A ROCK STAR. I WILL BE A LEGEND.** 🗚

Gc
Game Changers

Mercury was the frontman and lead singer for rock band Queen. Considered one of the greatest stadium rock bands of all time, Queen scored several no.1 albums and singles internationally, including in the UK and the US. Freddie played no small part in their success; not only did he write some of their most famous hits, including 'Bohemian Rhapsody' and 'We are the Champions', but he is possibly one of the greatest frontmen in history. Mercury's operatic vocal range of four octaves, energetic performance style and raw charisma captivated audiences. Watch Queen's 15-minute slot at the 1985 UK Live Aid to see Mercury bring a crowd of 72,000 people under his spell in just a few verses. Mercury was not 'out' in his lifetime and enjoyed a brief romantic relationship (and lifelong friendship) with Mary Austin. However, the majority of his long-term relationships and flings were with men, notably hairdresser Jim Hutton, his partner of nine years. Tragically Freddie Mercury was a victim of the late-twentieth-century AIDS crisis, dying of AIDS-related illness in the 1990s aged 45.

33.

Gc
Game Changers

Elton John

Younger readers may not remember a time when Elton John was not an out gay performer; a living legend of high camp performance in a long-term marriage with children. In fact, Elton spent the first decade of his career in the closet. In the seventies and early eighties he was a glam rock legend, releasing seminal album *Goodbye Yellow Brick Road* and appearing in The Who's rock opera *Tommy*, alongside releasing a slew of hits such as 'Rocket Man', 'The Bitch is Back' and 'Don't Let the Sun Go Down On Me'. In 1976, at the height of his fame, he came out as bisexual and ten years later, as gay. His visibility as a gay musician during the years where it seemed impossible to be gay and successfully hold a public, mainstream career inspired many. Dedicated to helping his community, Elton set up the Elton John AIDS Foundation, which raises millions yearly to help combat AIDS.

b.1947

" THE GREAT THING ABOUT ROCK AND ROLL IS THAT SOMEONE LIKE ME CAN BE A STAR. "

Sylvester

1947–1988

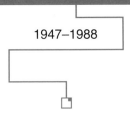

** SOMETIMES, FOLKS MAKE US FEEL STRANGE, BUT WE'RE NOT STRANGE. AND THOSE FOLKS – THEY'LL JUST HAVE TO CATCH UP. **

34.

Gc
Game Changers

The Cockettes were a San Franciscan avant garde art troupe known for their LSD-fuelled performances and flamboyant costumes that often played with gender boundaries. They counted celebrities such as Truman Capote among their fans and cult-favourite drag performer Divine (p.57) performed with them for a while. One of the Cockettes, Sylvester, broke onto the music scene with his disco hit 'You Make Me Feel (Mighty Real)'. Sylvester was openly gay, used both male and female pronouns and played with his gender presentation throughout his life; something the mainstream music business struggled to accept in the 1970s. He never withdrew from his roots, playing Prides around the world throughout his career. He campaigned in his lifetime for better AIDS treatments and, on his premature death from AIDS-related illness, left the proceeds of his music to two HIV/AIDS charities: Project Open Hand and the AIDS Emergency Fund.

35.

Gc
Game Changers

Sylvia Rivera was a woman of incredible strength and fortitude. She had to fend for herself from the age of 10, and was often homeless and participated in sex work in order to survive. She fought all her life for her rights and the rights of others; she lived openly as a transwoman, she was one of the LGBTQ+ people at the Stonewall Inn who fought back on the night of the riots and she helped organise the subsequent Christopher Street Liberation Day parade (that would later become Gay Pride). She founded STAR (Street Transvestite Action Revolutionaries), a shelter for homeless trans teens, with Marsha P. Johnson. She campaigned within the queer community for the inclusion of trans people; her famous speech at the 1973 Christopher Street Liberation Day rally highlights the battle trans people were facing to get any support from the queer community. The speech is available to view online and is one of the most powerful moments in queer history; despite being booed as she takes to the stage, with raw power and emotion she challenges the crowd, describing her violent and isolated experiences in frank terms until at the end the crowd is cheering and chanting 'gay power' with her.

Sylvia Rivera

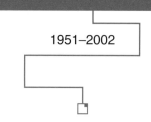

1951–2002

❝ I'M NOT MISSING A MINUTE OF THIS. IT'S A REVOLUTION! ❞

Peter Tatchell

b.1952

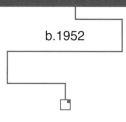

❝ BE SCEPTICAL, QUESTION AUTHORITY, BE A REBEL. DO NOT CONFORM AND DON'T BE ORDINARY. ❞

36.

Gc
Game Changers

Peter Tatchell is one of the UK's most prominent human rights and gay rights campaigners. Although it is hard to capture the full breadth of everything Tatchell has fought for in just a few words, career highlights include organising the UK's first gay Pride march, protesting in Russia against recent draconian homophobic laws, publishing a book – *Democratic Defence* – in favour of nuclear disarmament and twice attempting a citizen's arrest on Zimbabwean dictator Robert Mugabe. Tatchell has often experienced violence as a result of his protests and even, during a campaign for a Labour seat, received a live bullet through his letterbox. Undeterred, he has dedicated his life to campaigning for a better world; he recently lobbied UK Prime Minister Theresa May to apologise for Britain's imposition of anti-gay laws on Commonwealth countries during the nineteenth century (36 of the 53 Commonwealth countries still outlaw same-sex relations as a direct result of these laws). She did.

37.

Gc
Game Changers

Winterson's debut novel *Oranges Are Not the Only Fruit*, published in 1985 when she was only 26, is a coming-of-age tale of a young girl growing up in a fundamental Christian household. It follows her journey as she explores her faith, her sexuality and her place in society. It was an incredible success on release, winning the Whitbread Book Award for a first novel, and has since become required reading on the English Literature curriculum, establishing a place in the literary world for literature that explores the lives of gay people. The story was semi-autobiographical; Winterson had herself grown up in a fundamentalist Christian household, leaving home at 16 after coming out as a lesbian. She was accepted to Oxford University, supporting herself with part-time work while she gained her degree. Her follow-up novels achieved similar acclaim, particularly magical realist tale *Sexing the Cherry* and historical novel *The Passion*. Her mastery of writing across different genres secured her a place in the pantheon of modern literary greats. She is married to Susie Orbach, author of *Fat is a Feminist Issue*.

Jeanette Winterson

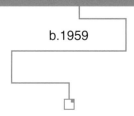

b.1959

❝ I AM A WRITER WHO HAPPENS TO LOVE WOMEN. I AM NOT A LESBIAN WHO HAPPENS TO WRITE. ❞

Pete Burns

1959–2016

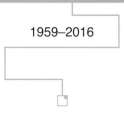
38.

Gc
Game Changers

Pete Burns shot to fame as the lead singer in 1980s pop band Dead or Alive. Their single 'You Spin Me Round (Like a Record)' reached number one on the UK singles chart and the top twenty in the US. Throughout his career Burns embraced his queer identity, exploring queer themes in his music. MTV banned the video for Dead or Alive's single 'I'll Save You All My Kisses' due to its queer content; the video featured Burns dressed in tights and a leather jacket dancing on a baseball diamond while shirtless men crowded around a chain-link fence, starling longingly at him. Later in life, Burns played with his gender presentation, altering his appearance through cosmetic surgery. In his lifetime he was married twice, once to Lynne Corlett and then once holding a civil partnership with Michael Simpson. Of his identity and presentation Burns commented, '[People] always want to know – am I gay, bi, trans or what? I say, forget all that... I'm just Pete.'

RuPaul

b.1960

39.

Gc
Game Changers

RuPaul came up on the Atlanta club scene, working for years as a genderfuck (androgynous) drag artist. He hit the big time in 1993 when he released a single, 'Supermodel (You Betta Work)'. It was a massive club hit and launched RuPaul to a level of fame unprecedented for a drag queen in America. An iconic photo shows him with Nirvana, holding a young Frances Bean Cobain, at that year's MTV VMA awards. Having eschewed genderfuck for full glamour, Rupaul gained a modelling contract with MAC Cosmetics. His career went from strength to strength, with him getting his own talk show on MTV and playing bit parts in films such as *The Brady Bunch*, until, in 2009, he launched *RuPaul's Drag Race*. The show pits drag queens against each other to take the title of 'America's Next Drag Superstar'. Originally intended to be a spoof take on reality shows such as *America's Next Top Model*, *Drag Race* has soared in popularity. At the time of writing the show holds nine Emmy awards and is on its tenth season (not including three all-star seasons), having launched the global career of over 100 drag artists and spawned several drag conventions. Drag artistry, previously a niche even in LGBT culture, has become a global sensation. Former *Drag Race* alums are signed to modelling agencies in their drag personas, have successful films on Netflix and have been featured in reality shows such as *Celebrity Big Brother* and *Scared Famous*. Ironically, after having famously said 'Drag will never be mainstream', RuPaul is responsible for having made drag a global sensation.

❝ IF YOU CAN'T LOVE YOURSELF HOW THE HELL YOU GONNA LOVE SOMEONE ELSE? ❞

40. Gc
Game Changers

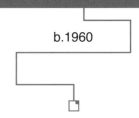

Alison Bechdel

b.1960

Alison Bechdel is a writer and illustrator whose graphic novel memoirs are critically acclaimed. Her first memoir, *Fun Home*, written about the experience of accepting her sexuality at the same time as realising her dad was gay, was lauded on release. *Fun Home* was later adapted into a musical, winning five Tony Awards, including the coveted 'Best Musical'. You may recognise her name best from the Bechdel-Wallace test (sometimes known as the Bechdel Test). This is a quick way to work out whether a film has even entry-level representation of female characters. The three criteria a film must pass are: are there at least two female characters, are they both named, and do they share a conversation about something other than a man? Bechdel credits her friend Liz Wallace with the idea, which she first presented as a strip in her comic *Dykes to Watch Out For* (p.111). The strip itself has run since the 1980s and is essential queer culture reading.

" FEMINISM IS THE THEORY. LESBIANISM IS THE PRACTICE. "

Eddie Izzard

b.1962

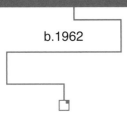

THEY'RE NOT WOMEN'S CLOTHES. THEY'RE MY CLOTHES. I BOUGHT THEM.

41.

Gc
Game Changers

Eddie Izzard built his career as an accomplished stand-up, famous for surrealist flights of fancy and whimsy. Early on in his career he identified as a 'straight transvestite', often performing in make-up, nail polish or so-called 'women's clothes' (sorry, Eddie). Although he would talk about his outfit as part of his act, the clothes weren't a gimmick but an extension of his everyday outfits and expression of his identity. Izzard has identified variously as a straight transvestite, a male lesbian, transgender and 'a complete boy plus half a girl' in his lifetime (his pronouns remain he/him). A talented linguist as well as comedian, Izzard has performed his set in French, German, Arabic, Spanish and Russian. He has completed several impressive physical feats, too, running seven marathons in seven days and 43 marathons in 51 days for Sports Relief. Izzard has now turned his hand to politics, campaigning for UK political party Labour, and holding a seat on the Labour National Executive.

Gc

42.

Game Changers

After springing to fame with his band *Wham!* at the age of 19 and for some years being the biggest pop star of the 1980s (who can get through the festive season without hearing 'Last Christmas'?), George Michael experienced a moment that was to define his career and his life for the years to come. In 1998 he was arrested for apparently engaging in a lewd act in a public toilet with what turned out to be an undercover police officer. The arrest and the subsequent media attention outed him to the public. Although suffering intense media scrutiny due to the arrest, Michael kept his head high, and later that year released the single 'Outside', which took a comedic swipe at his arrest and sentence. Michael became a figure who refused to allow others to shame him for his sexuality, and his career enjoyed a renaissance. Sadly, after being troubled for some years by ill health, Michael died in 2016 aged only 53. After his death many charities, including Childline, the Terrence Higgins Trust and Macmillan Cancer Support, revealed that he had been quietly donating millions to their causes over the years.

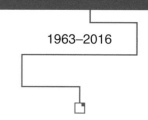

George Michael

1963–2016

❝ I WANT PEOPLE TO KNOW THAT I HAVE NOT BEEN EXPOSED AS A GAY MAN IN ANY WAY THAT I FEEL ANY SHAME FOR. ❞

Dan Savage

b.1964

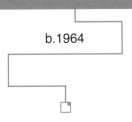

> **IT GETS BETTER. HOWEVER BAD IT IS NOW, IT GETS BETTER. AND IT CAN GET GREAT, IT CAN GET AWESOME.**

43.

Dan Savage has leveraged his voice as an irreverent advice columnist specialising in frank advice about sexuality into a nationally recognised campaign for LGBTQ+ rights. His column, Savage Love, started life as a joke, offering flippant advice to heterosexual letter writers as a play on the awful advice queer advice-seekers would receive in mainstream advice columns. However, Savage was just too good at his job and his fresh outlook on sex, kink and relationships made his column a hit. He has popularised many sex and relationship terms; notably the use of 'pegging' (the word was the winner of a reader's poll to pick the best name for the act) and 'santorum' (a word for the by-product of anal sex) after homophobic US Senator Rick Santorum. In 2010 Savage and his husband Terry Miller founded the It Gets Better Project, a series of video testimonials uploaded online from LGBTQ+ community members that discuss their happy lives. The project was created in response to a series of suicides by queer teens who had been bullied after coming out. There are now over 50,000 participants, including celebrities such as Jane Lynch, Zachary Quinto, Ellen DeGeneres, Adam Lambert and Neil Patrick Harris.

44.

Gc
Game Changers

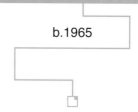

Alan Cumming

b.1965

Alan Cumming's acting career is as varied as it is successful. Only three years after his 1998 Tony-award-wining portrayal of the Master of Ceremonies in *Cabaret* on Broadway, Cumming acted the villain in the childhood favourite *Spy Kids* film. He has similarly turned his hand to costume drama, comedy, TV and authorship, becoming one of today's most beloved character actors; in addition to his Tony Award Cummings holds an Olivier Award for his work in the 1990 Royal National Theatre production of *Accidental Death of an Anarchist*. Cumming is openly bisexual and is married to illustrator Grant Shaffer. He is almost as famous for his sparkling personality and wit as he is for his accomplished career. Cumming has released two fragrances: the first is named 'Cumming' and the second '2nd (Alan) Cumming'; the proceeds of the second fragrance all go to charity. In 2009 he was awarded an OBE for his services to theatre and for his work campaigning for LGBT rights – he has campaigned for charities such as GLAAD, The Trevor Project and the Matthew Shepard Foundation. A proud Scotsman, Cumming attended the ceremony in a tartan kilt suit.

❝ I NEVER FELT ANY SHAME ABOUT MY SEXUALITY AND THE IDEA I FOUND BOYS ATTRACTIVE AS WELL AS GIRLS. ❞

Sarah Waters

b.1966

" I'M INTERESTED IN STORIES THAT AREN'T GETTING TOLD: IT'S WHERE MY INTERESTS LIE. "

45.

Sarah Waters' twisting, sensual historical fiction has catapulted her to success. Her debut novel, *Tipping the Velvet* (titled after an obscure Victorian term for cunnilingus), tells the story of a young female oyster seller in 1890s Whitstable, UK, who falls for a male impersonator and follows her to London to find fame, love and misadventure. It was a smash on release in 1998, lauded for its humour, vivacity and its frank portrayal of lesbian desire and sex. These have become Waters' trademarks; she recognises that her books establish a new literary tradition of historical literary fiction that acknowledges lesbian lives and loves. Her work has been adapted for the screen several times; *Tipping the Velvet* and *Fingersmith* were adapted as BBC miniseries, *Fingersmith* was adapted by Park Chan-wook as the Korean film *The Handmaiden*, and *The Little Stranger* has also been adapted for film.

Gc
46.
Game Changers

Ruth Hunt is CEO of the UK-based charity Stonewall, the largest organisation of its kind in Europe. On her first day as head of the organisation she announced that Stonewall would expand to include trans rights in its remit, having previously focussed on gay, lesbian and bisexual rights only. The organisation now campaigns for trans rights, including pushing to update the Gender Recognition Act, which came into effect in 2005, to allow trans people to self-identify their gender. Hunt began her career as an LGBTQ+ activist at a young age, writing advice columns for the lesbian magazine *DIVA* (who accidentally outed her to her parents when they rang her landline about work) from the age of 15. She went on to become Oxford University Student Union's first lesbian president and worked in the public sector for several years before helming Stonewall.

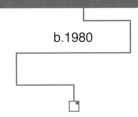

Ruth Hunt

b.1980

"PEOPLE USED TO ASK ME HOW I KNEW I WAS A LESBIAN. MY ANSWER: HOW DO YOU KNOW YOU'RE STRAIGHT?"

Juno Dawson

b.1981

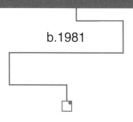

> ❝ I DARE TO DREAM OF A WORLD WHERE PEOPLE CAN DRESS, SPEAK AND BEHAVE HOW THEY WANT, FREE FROM MOCKERY, DERISION, JUDGEMENT, HARASSMENT AND DANGER. ❞

47.

Gc
Game Changers

Dawson was already a big-name YA author when she came out publicly as transgender. She was crowned 'Queen of Teen' at the 2014 YA book awards. Her work was commended for featuring LGBTQ+ themes, including hit non-fiction work *This Book is Gay*, a YA exploration of what gender and sexuality means. Coming out while famous meant she would be subject to even more scrutiny than the already high amount trans people receive, but she knew it was the right thing for her. Since her transition Dawson's career has continued to grow; she published a non-fiction work *The Gender Games: The Problem with Men and Women... From Someone Who Has Been Both* and a novel *Clean*, about a teen socialite dealing with addiction (the television rights for both books have been acquired by production companies). Since coming out as trans Dawson has also spoken openly and frankly about her experience in national publications such as *The Guardian* and programs such as BBC *Women's Hour*, *ITV News* and *This Morning*.

48.

Gc
Game Changers

Janet Mock is a journalist, bestselling author and transgender rights campaigner. She started her career as an editor for the magazine *People* before coming out publicly in a *Marie Claire* article which was written by another journalist in her voice and given the headline 'I was born a boy'. Mock protested the title and her representation in the article, as her assigned gender at birth didn't match her true gender identity as a girl. She said, 'My genital reconstructive surgery did not make me a girl. I was always a girl.' Her autobiography, *Redefining Realness*, was a *New York Times* bestseller and helped launch her career as a media advocate and television presenter. Today she is an authoritative voice for trans people and trans people of colour. She made history in 2018 as the first trans woman of colour to be hired as a TV writer when she joined the team for *Pose*, a series set in the 1980s New York ball scene.

Janet Mock

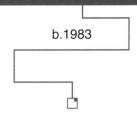

b.1983

❝ I BELIEVE THAT TELLING OUR STORIES, FIRST TO OURSELVES AND THEN TO ONE ANOTHER AND THE WORLD, IS A REVOLUTIONARY ACT. ❞

Laverne Cox

b.1984

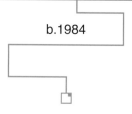

> **AS LONG AS WE ARE LIVING IN A CULTURE WHERE ONE HAS TO PROVE THEIR WOMANHOOD OR MANHOOD, WE ARE NOT LIVING IN A FREE CULTURE.**

49.

Laverne Cox first came to national attention when she appeared on the reality TV show *I Want to Work for Diddy*. She was an out trans woman at the time, the first out trans woman to appear on a reality show, and her role helped win the show a GLAAD award (GLAAD is an LGBTQ+ company that monitors LGBTQ+ representation in the media) for Outstanding Reality Series. Although she did not win, her tenure was so successful that the channel VH1 approached Cox about starring in her own show. Cox produced and starred in *TRANSform Me*, a show in which trans women would give makeover advice to cis women. Although it was cancelled, Cox's TV career was launched. After several bit roles in TV shows Cox landed the part of transwoman Sophia Burset in Netflix's hit prison dramedy *Orange is the New Black*. Since taking up the role she has become the first openly trans person to be nominated for an Emmy award in the acting category and the first openly trans person to appear on the cover of *TIME*, raising the profile of successful trans people in the US.

50.

Gc
Game Changers

Ellen Page

b.1987

Indie darling Ellen Page has acted since childhood and found fame in cult classics such as *Juno* (for which she was nominated for an Oscar) and the thriller *Hard Candy*. She was one of the biggest contemporary film stars when, in 2014, she came out in a speech at the Human Rights Campaign's Time to Thrive conference. The conference aims to promote safety and well-being for LGBTQ+ children around the globe, to tackle problems such as the fact that only 26 per cent of LGBTQ+ teens feel safe in their classrooms. In her speech to the conference Page condemned the gender limitations imposed on people by society as well as publicly announcing for the first time that she was gay. Page is one of the few A-list female actors to come out at the height of their fame, knowingly risking her career to defend LGBTQ+ rights. In addition to her A-list acting she presents Viceland's series *Gaycation*, an exploration of queer culture around the world.

❛❛ I'M HAPPIER THAN I PROBABLY COULD IMAGINE. NOW IT DOESN'T FEEL LIKE I WAS EVER NOT OUT. ❜❜

Jack Monroe

b.1988

I'M A LITTLE BIT FEMALE AND A LITTLE BIT MALE.

51.

Gc
Game Changers

As a single parent receiving government benefits Jack Monroe was forced to budget only £10 a week for food to feed themselves and their young son. Their blog, now called Cooking on a Bootstrap, charted their attempts to remain in-budget and cook healthy and delicious food. The blog was a hit in austerity-stricken Britain and Monroe rose to fame, publishing a cookbook called *A Girl Called Jack*. Monroe has been vocal against government spending cuts that hit the UK's poor the hardest and has worked with charities such as Unite the Union, Oxfam and the Child Poverty Action Group to campaign against poverty. They identify as a lesbian and non-binary, coming out as genderqueer while in the public eye. Monroe's frank discussions around their body and gender identity have opened up the media conversation and perception of what it is to be gender nonconforming – *The Guardian* calls them the first UK celebrity to come out as genderqueer.

Gc
52.
Game Changers

In the late 1980s and early 1990s LGBT activists in New York noted a sharp rise in street violence against queer people. One activist group, Queer Nation, campaigned against this with the slogan 'gays bash back'. A portion of Queer Nation formed the Pink Panther Patrol (a rejected alternative name was The Lavender Berets), a group that would patrol New York's West Village and protect its queer inhabitants from homophobic violence. The initiative was popular; soon after the group had formed over 150 people volunteered to participate. They would train volunteers in how to patrol an area effectively; one member of each patrol would act as a legal observer (taking note of details that would help in any potential court cases), another would call the police upon spotting trouble and if they needed to intervene they would run in to a violent situation blowing their whistles and disperse the violence. New York was not the only city where queer people banded together to protect themselves on the street; patrols also formed in Houston, Dallas, San Francisco, Los Angeles, Kansas City, Philadelphia, Boston and Seattle.

The Pink Panthers Patrol

Various, c.1990

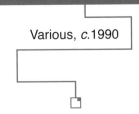

❝ OUR MESSAGE IS WE'RE BASHING BACK. ❞

Chapter 6:
It's a Celebration!

The term 'Pride' was first used in 1967 by a group calling themselves Personal Rights in Defense and Education (PRIDE). They were protesting outside the Black Cat Tavern in Los Angeles, which had been subject to a series of increasingly brutal raids by the LAPD, including a particularly cruel raid on New Year's Eve when plain-clothed officers waited until the queer patrons were kissing to celebrate the new year to burst in and violently arrest them. They also raised funds for those arrested on that night and ran a newsletter which blossomed into *The Advocate*. Although PRIDE eventually dissolved, the name was catchy and embodied the values those marching for gay liberation wished to promote. (It should be noted that SCCRH, Southern California Council on Religion and Homophile, also protested outside the Black Cat Tavern, although sadly 'Gay Sccrh' never caught on.) Since those first embattled years, the Pride movement has developed and grown across the world. Festivals celebrating queer culture have spun off from the original days of marching for liberation and now you can as easily find queer Oktoberfests as you can a Pride celebration in your local area. Here are a few of the world's biggest, brightest and most unusual queer celebrations.

53.

C
Celebrations

Come 1970 and the Stonewall riots of the year before had stirred something in America's (and the world's) queer communities. On 27 June Chicago held a week-long celebration, which culminated in a march of around 150 people from Washington Center to the Civic Center. They titled it the 'Gay Liberation March' and their slogan was 'Gay Power'. The next day two separately organised marches took place in New York and Los Angeles, the former called The Christopher Street Liberation Day Parade and the latter organised by the Christopher Street West Organization (both named after Christopher Street, the location of the Stonewall Inn). The marchers would chant, shouting that they were 'gay and proud'. As queer culture developed over the years, and more cities across the US and the world were adopting marches, organisers would switch the name of their marches from liberation days to Pride.

The First Pride Parade

27 June 1970–present

Chicago, USA

The UK's First Pride

1 July 1972–present

London, UK

54.

The first UK Pride was organised by Peter Tatchell and took place in London in 1972. The UK Gay Pride Rally was attended by around 2,000 people. London continued to hold yearly events; by 1978 there was an official Pride Week and by the early 2000s London Pride was one of the biggest Pride celebrations worldwide. Other UK cities had soon followed suit; Brighton, the UK's famous LGBTQ+-friendly town, held their inaugural Pride event in 1973. In the north of England, Manchester Pride is one of the country's longest-running Pride events, having run since the mid-1980s. The event takes place near Manchester's famous Canal Street, the setting of the original UK version of TV series *Queer as Folk* (see p.118).

55.

C
Celebrations

The Gay Games

28 August 1982–present

San Francisco, USA

Athletes and sportspeople worldwide have found that openness about their sexuality has not benefited their career. Founder of the Gay Games, Tom Waddell, a gay decathlete, was disillusioned after competing in the 1968 Summer Olympics, noting a disheartening amount of institutionalised racism, homophobia, sexism and nationalism. He sought to create an international sporting event that would be inclusive of everyone and, in 1982, launched the inaugural Gay Games in San Francisco. Tina Turner performed at the opening ceremony and over 1,300 participants competed in a range of events. By the third games in 1990 over 7,000 athletes were taking part and, come the 2018 Gay Games in Paris, over 10,000 people travelled from all over the world to compete. The Gay Games' inclusivity is something to be relished: they hosted the first international women's wrestling competition in 1994; trans athletes are welcome to take part and to compete as the gender they live, without any gender policing; and, in a testament to inclusivity, even heterosexual athletes are encouraged to participate.

Wigstock

1984–2000, 2018–present

New York City, USA

Riffing on the famous 1969 music festival Woodstock, Wigstock is an annual outdoor drag festival. Created by drag legend Lady Bunny, Wigstock ran from 1984 to 2000, and was then revived in 2018 as drag became an international sensation. The festival was a drag institution, regularly featuring drag superstars and queer icons such as RuPaul, Jackie Beat, Lypsinka, Leigh Bowery, Amanda Lepore, Sherry Vine and Candis Cayne. The first, almost impromptu festival (the creators claim it came about after a drunk decision to hold a drag festival) was attended by around 1,000 people and numbers swelled every year, until, in 1997, Wigstock raised over $30,000 for Gay Men's Health Crisis. A documentary capturing the 1995 Wigstock, titled *Wigstock: The Movie*, was released that same year – essential viewing for fans of queer and drag history.

57.

C
Celebrations

The Black and Blue Festival is a dance festival held in Montreal over Canadian Thanksgiving weekend. The festival is run by Bad Boy Club Montreal, a charitable organisation dedicated to raising money for HIV and AIDS charities as well as directly supporting people living with HIV/AIDS in Montreal. The festival consists of a wide variety of events in venues around the city, including brunches, cocktail parties and sporting activities. The biggest feature of the festival circuit, however, is the balls, usually in the form of all-night raves, culminating in the Black and Blue Main Event on Sunday and the Recovery Party on Monday. Other previous themes have included Chrome Party and The Leather Ball – Solid Chrome Edition. The festival's roster of DJs are internationally acclaimed and attendance reaches around 75,000.

Black and Blue Festival

October 1991–present

Montreal, Canada

EuroGames

1992–present

Europe

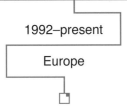

58.

C
Celebrations

The EuroGames is an international sporting event open to everyone who wishes to compete 'regardless of gender, age, race, gender identity or sexual orientation'. Even non-Europeans are welcome to join, provided that all Europeans who wish to enter have been registered and there are still spots available! The games are organised by the EGLSF, the European Gay and Lesbian Sports Federation, and their aim is to bring high-quality sports to queer people around Europe. The games even has its own anthem, 'We Are Leaving', presented at the 1996 Berlin EuroGames. Three thousand participants competed in the 2016 EuroGames, held in Helsinki, in sports as diverse as a Pride run, basketball, swimming, dance, bridge and bowling. Categories in competitions such as dance are diverse: there are several senior options as well as group, couple and solo competitions (all couples must be same sex).

59.

C
Celebrations

Organising and advertising a Pride event is no small feat, especially in areas where there isn't a large 'out' queer population, or where the queer population may not feel safe in expressing their queerness on the streets. Three cheers, then, for organisations that lend money and logistics to such queer communities. In the UK, the organisation UK Pride chooses a different Pride each year to magnify, opting to 'shine a beacon' on Pride events that may not usually achieve national attention. Recent recipients of UK Pride include the small Isle of Wight Pride, only in its second year, and Pride in Hull, which achieved a five-fold increase in attendance. WorldPride works with already large-scale Pride events to bring an even higher level of coverage and celebration. For example, Toronto city council reported that WorldPride brought in around six times the revenue that Toronto Pride usually generated. EuroPride works in much the same way, on a European level.

UK Pride, EuroPride and WorldPride

1992 onwards

Worldwide

Glasgay! and SQIFF

1993–2014

Glasgow, UK

60.

The Glasgay! festival ran for over 20 years and is in itself a representation of the development of queer culture. It was founded in 1993, but Glasgow City Council attempted to prevent the festival from taking place before it had even had its inaugural run. By its last run in 2014, Glasgow City Council was one of Glasgay!'s biggest sponsors. The 30-day cultural event featured comedy, theatre, art exhibitions, film and clubbing and paved the way for many queer festivals in the UK. For those looking for current queer events in Scotland, SQIFF, or the Scottish Queer International Film Festival, has run in Glasgow from 2015. In addition to their queer-focussed programming, SQIFF has been working to ensure accessibility to its events, recognising that for those in the margins attending a film festival may be a luxury. Following the lead of Leeds Queer Film Festival, SQIFF introduced a sliding scale, allowing their audience to pay anything from nothing to £8 according to their self-evaluated financial status. The response was definitive; SQIFF reported an increase of 45 per cent in audience numbers and 69 per cent in box office takings.

61.

C
Celebrations

LesGaiCineMad

8 November 1996–present

Madrid, Spain

LesGaiCineMad, titled after 'Lesbico, Gai, Cinema, Madrid', is a festival of queer Spanish-speaking films held annually in Madrid. It's Madrid's biggest cultural festival, attended by around 14,000 people, and gives cash prizes for a variety of awards including Best Film Directed By a Woman, Best Documentary and Best Experimental Short Film. Recently the organisation has also run the Madrid Lesbian Film Festival in May, to highlight work by and featuring lesbian, bisexual and queer women, citing cinema's need to represent these women in non-stereotypical ways. They also run the Latin American LGBT Film Network, which brings queer film festivals to Spanish-speaking countries around the world, such as the Dominican Santo Domingo OutFest, Guatemalan La Otra Banqueta, Panamanian Diverso Festival, Colombian Pink Cycle, Ecuadorian El Lugar Sin Limites and Chilean Movilh. This work not only unites queer audiences with queer cinema but showcases work by queer filmmakers, granting them access to powerful people such as financers, distributers and international film festival programmers.

Seoul Queer Culture Festival

2000–present

Seoul, Korea

The Seoul Queer Culture Festival is the country's longest-running queer culture festival (although the only other is the Deagu Queer Culture Festival), having taken place annually since 2000. It usually runs for around two weeks and sometimes includes a Pride march and a film festival; recent figures show attendance at around 120,000 people. Although it is well attended and boasts a rich programme of events, the festival has run into troubles: many attendees sport glasses and a face mask to hide their identity, as some homophobic harassers distribute photographs of attendants in order to shame them. In 2014 the regime withdrew governmental support and in 2015 the festival was banned from continuing, although it resumed in 2016 after the Human Rights Watch condemned this action in a letter.

63.

C
Celebrations

Beijing Queer Film Festival

2001–present

Beijing, China

The Beijing Queer Film Festival is a direct challenge to China's censorship laws, which order that there must be no positive depiction of trans, gay, lesbian or bisexual lives in the media. Although homosexuality is not criminalised, there are no laws protecting queer people from discrimination and they are legislated against using that old chestnut of an excuse – representation of LGBTQ+ lives is queer 'propaganda'. As a result the film festival may not use mainstream venues and has been shut down several times over its near twenty years of existence. Despite this adversity the Beijing Queer Film Festival persists in its great work bringing a spectrum of international LGBTQ+ films to China, where even such mainstream films as *Brokeback Mountain* are only available on the black market. Although queer people in China face government-sanctioned discrimination, they continue to fight for a space for themselves; in 2017 Shanghai followed Beijing's lead and launched the Shanghai Queer Film Festival.

The World's Biggest Pride Parade

2006–present

Sao Paulo, Brazil

64.

Celebrations

Sao Paulo Pride Parade lays claim to being the world's biggest Pride parade, reporting its numbers at around three million. However, due to the federal police's (who officially run crowd control for the event) refusal to confirm official figures, Sao Paulo is unable to throw its crown in the ring and claim the title. Sao Paulo may not have the official blessing but that doesn't seem to have affected turnout; millions attended in 2018, with the slogan: 'Power for the LGBTQ+ – Our Vote, Our Voice!' Madrid's 2017 Pride, the year it hosted WorldPride, holds the record for highest reported attendance; the organisation logged three and a half million, with the city authorities reporting two and a half million celebrants. New York City Pride is possibly the Pride event that most regularly reports the highest numbers of celebrants, clocking in at over two million.

65.

C
Celebrations

Arts charity Wise Thoughts has run London-based queer art festival GFest, or Gaywise FESTival for over 10 years, developing it into an internationally-renowned 'art festival for all'. GFest showcases a wide spectrum of works, including poetry, music, performances, art exhibitions, interdisciplinary art and debates in a series of venues across London, including the Tate Modern, Gay's the Word bookshop (the UK's only bookshop focussing on queer literature) and the National Theatre. It is supported by the government, commonly receiving messages of support from the London Mayor and endorsements by MPs and celebrities. Recent themes include 'Socially Equal', 'Arts Protest' and 'OUT [in the margins]'. The festival is attended by thousands each year.

GFest Arts Festival

November 2007–present

London, UK

Delhi Queer Pride Parade

30 June 2008–present

Delhi, India

66.

Delhi held their inaugural Pride in 2008, while homosexual acts were still ruled illegal in India under Section 377. Although it was quietly attended at first, by the end of the day over 500 people were gathered, chanting to repeal Section 377. Attendance grew over the years and in 2016 a crowd of around 1,000 people was recorded. Attending a gay Pride parade in a country that rules homosexual acts illegal is an act of incredible bravery. Section 377 was finally repealed in 2009, after having been brought to India in 1861 under rule of the British Empire. Sadly, the legislation was reintroduced in 2013. However, as of 2018 LGBTQ+ campaigners' persistence paid off when Section 377 was repealed again.

67.

C
Celebrations

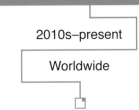

New Pride

2010s–present

Worldwide

As Pride spreads across the world, new places are taking up the rainbow flag. Georgetown, Guyana, held their inaugural Pride march in 2018, despite Guyana being the only country in South America where homosexuality is illegal. In June of 2018 Pride celebrations took place at a research station in Antarctica, the first of their kind to take place at the South Pole. It was attended by 10 people, which may not sound much but is a mighty ten per cent of Antarctica's winter population. Early in 2018 the Indian city Ahmedabad held its first Pride celebration while the country waited to hear whether homosexual activity would be decriminalised (it was, later in the year). The Kakuma Refugee Camp in northwestern Kenya held its first Pride event in 2018, which was attended by a 600-strong crowd. Many of the LGBTQ+ refugees at the camp had fled from persecution based on their sexuality or gender identity.

The Pink Weiner Wiesn Festival

2012–present

Vienna, Austria

C

The Pink Weiner Wiesn Festival has run in Vienna for over five years as part of the Wiener Wiesn-Fest, providing queer lovers of lederhosen, dirndl and beer with an alternative way to celebrate. If you enjoy Oktoberfest-style fun you can join the Pink Weiner Wiesn Festival tent for a night of music, comedy, drag and hearty food and then go again in the morning for a *Frühschoppen*, or morning pint. The crowd is encouraged to dress up and sing and dance along for a night of raucous enjoyment. There has long been a tradition of 'Gay Sundays' for Oktoberfests in Germany and Austria. Munich's 'Gay Sunday', Rosa Wiesn, is one of the biggest events in the Munich queer calendar. It is attended by thousands and has recently expanded to include two other days, Rosl Montag and Prosecco-Wiesn. Other countries have taken up the queer Oktoberfest mantle, too; events in London include Pink Oktoberfest and Queer-Schenke Oktoberfest.

Chapter 7:
The Arts

We humans create art as a way to tell stories and express ourselves, which reaffirms our identities and our cultural values and allows us to experience events that we may never otherwise do in our lifetimes. Marginalised groups such as the queer community often suffer from being excluded from mainstream art; not seeing any stories about ourselves or else seeing negative or limited portrayals of our existence that don't fit with our own understanding of ourselves as complex human beings. This isn't from lack of creativity and creation but from lack of exposure; the queer community has created enduring works of high and low art that speak to our hearts, humour and humanity. We have created timeless love stories, side-stitching comedies, revealing documentaries, gritty social portraits and everything in between. Here are some queer works of art, some forgotten and some famous, that reflect us in all our glory, as complicated, sometimes-messy, sometimes-heroic, wonderful humans.

The Picture of Dorian Gray

1890

Novel

69.

Ta
The Arts

The queer content in *The Picture of Dorian Gray* is mostly subtextual, although there was enough in there to be used against Oscar Wilde in his prosecution for gross indecency. The first edition of the novel was considered scandalous by Victorian society, so much so that Wilde rewrote sections in order to insert more general moralistic sentiments and cloud the more homoerotic moments. The revised edition particularly lost some of the more overt statements of love between male characters and references to their having any feminine qualities. Whatever it lost in the rewrite, it remains one of the finest works in the English language; a compelling tale of decadence, sensuality, morality and society, all written with Wilde's typical wit but with a deeper sincerity and beauty, too.

Maurice

1913 (written);
1971 (published);
1987 (movie)

Novel and movie

Ta
The Arts

70.

Maurice was the last work of celebrated novelist E. M. Forster to be published. Although he wrote it in 1913, Forster considered the novel, a tale of gay love, unpublishable and it was only published posthumously in 1971. Forster was himself gay and for much of his lifetime in the UK homosexuality was not only illegal but aggressively prosecuted. The novel's initial reception was mixed, but, having had astonishing success with several other Forster screen adaptations, filmmaking team Ismail Merchant and James Ivory decided to make a film of the book in 1987. Merchant and Ivory were not only successful filmmakers – their studio Merchant Ivory Productions has produced over 40 films and the Guinness World Records reports them as the world's longest film partnership – but life partners. A young Hugh Grant, in only his second film role, played main character's first love interest, Clive. *Maurice* was an international and critical success. One of its most radical elements was its happy ending; it often seems that queer films need to have an element of tragedy about them to achieve some mainstream success: mainstream audiences prefer their LGBTQ+ heroes to suffer nobly. *Maurice* was released at the height of the AIDS epidemic and portrayed a gay hero who found his glossy, romantic 'happily ever after'; a truly radical act for the time. Ivory, who remained with Merchant until Merchant's death in 2005, would go on to win an Oscar for his screen adaptation of *Call Me By Your Name* in 2018, another queer coming-of-age tale.

71.

Ta
The Arts

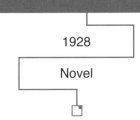

The Well of Loneliness

1928

Novel

Author Radclyffe Hall referred to herself as an 'invert', a late-nineteenth- and early-twentieth-century term for a gay person. She lived with Mabel Batten until Batten died, and then with Una, Lady Troubridge for the rest of her life. She published *The Well of Loneliness*, her only book to explore queer themes, in 1928 to much uproar: the book was the subject of an obscenity trial and all copies were ordered to be destroyed. Despite this, it was reprinted over the years and became a queer classic, one of the earliest novels to portray lesbian love. The lead character, a woman named Stephen, finds love with various women but the couples struggle to find a place in society that accepts them. Nonetheless, Stephen is an energetic and worthy protagonist, being awarded a medal for bravery during World War One and enjoying a successful career as an author. She seeks to change society rather than herself and utters the immortal plea 'Give us also the right to our existence!', an early gay rights credo.

Orlando

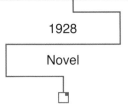

1928

Novel

72.

Ta
The Arts

Orlando has been called 'the longest and most charming love letter in literature'. Inspired by author Virginia Woolf's lover Vita Sackville-West, it is the sprawling tale of the immortal Orlando, who adventures through English history, first as one gender, then another. Orlando's body changes only once but they choose to live as different genders throughout their life and they love many people of different genders. *Orlando* is now considered one of the great works of English literature but don't let that put you off – it is also a romp, full of adventure, romance and satire. The film adaptation stars androgynous actor Tilda Swinton in the eponymous role and queer icon Quentin Crisp as Elizabeth I, under whose reign Orlando starts their journey.

73.

Ta
The Arts

Christopher Isherwood's novel is a semi-autobiographical tale of pre-World War Two Germany, drawn from his experiences living there. It is built of six short stories and novellas, one of which, 'Sally Bowles', introduced to the world the fabulous eponymous character. The classic queer film *Cabaret* was based on the novel, specifically the stories about Sally. 'On Ruegen Island' explores the lives of gay couple Otto and Peter, whose uncertain relationship is further complicated by the rise of the Nazi regime. Pre-war Berlin was one of the most liberal cities in Europe and Isherwood, who was openly gay himself, provides a snapshot of a queer city being encroached upon by a populist, hateful regime.

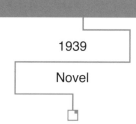

Goodbye to Berlin

1939

Novel

Nightwood

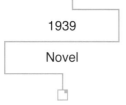

1939

Novel

Nightwood is a gothic novel written by modernist poet, essayist, playwright and author Djuna Barnes. Published in 1939, it is considered one of the earliest examples of lesbian literature and certainly one of the earliest books to contain an overt portrayal of attraction and love between women. As with most gothic novels, misery and tragedy does lurk behind most doorways, so this isn't one for those who prefer happy endings. It was a great hit in its time; William S. Burroughs referred to it as 'one of the great books of the twentieth century'. Barnes herself was a fascinating literary figure; she was friends with many literary and artistic greats of the day and once remarked to a friend that she 'had no feeling of guilt whatever about sex, about going to bed with any man or woman she wanted'. For a more light-hearted touch see Barnes' satirical novel *Ladies Almanack*, an illustrated volume cataloguing the sexual intrigues of thinly veiled versions of Barnes' lesbian friends and acquaintances.

75.

Ta
The Arts

Rubyfruit Jungle

1973

Novel

Rita Mae Brown's book *Rubyfruit Jungle* is a riot of language and sexuality. It explodes the traditional YA 'coming of age' story as teen Molly searches for her place in the world. Molly is a fantastic, irrepressible protagonist who, although she faces hardships as a result of society's reaction to her sexuality, doesn't question her own desires. She falls for several beautiful girls, and later women, in her life and pursues them, often successfully. *Rubyfruit Jungle* is a seminal work of literary fiction that has set the bar for queer coming-of-age tales and, although it was written nearly 50 years ago, it still resonates today.

The Rocky Horror Picture Show

1973 (musical);
1975 (movie)

Musical and movie

76.

Ta
The Arts

It is a tale as old as time; a drag queen's first time in drag is usually either on Halloween or attending a live screening of *The Rocky Horror Picture Show*. This film barely needs an introduction, such cult status has it developed over the years. Suffice to say it is a high camp musical romp through science fiction and horror tropes, bursting with sexuality, gender bending and quotable lines. *Rocky Horror* deserves every bit of its enduring fame, but if the film consisted only of Tim Curry's character Dr Frank N. Furter descending in a rickety elevator, clad in black lingerie and rhinestoned heels, then it would still be one of the best queer films in history. The US Library of Congress presumably agree, as they selected the film for preservation for cultural importance in 2005.

La Cage aux Folles

1973 (show);
1978 (movie)

Show and movie

Ta
The Arts

French actor and playwright Jean Poiret's delightful farce, *La Cage aux Folles*, is one of the most enduring queer texts of modern times. It's the story of a gay couple who pretend to be straight in order to impress their son's very conservative future in-laws. The body of the story is farce at its finest; ill-thought-out lies, mistaken identity, risky disguises, slapstick and escalating situations. The meat of the show is so very funny that the audience almost misses how radical (for the time – the play was first shown in 1973) the heart of the story is – a happy and successful queer nuclear family who eventually win the day over their bigoted heterosexual in-laws. The show was a smash hit on release and spawned several film adaptations. The first, released in 1978, is critically acclaimed and continues to be one of the top ten bestselling foreign films in the USA. An American adaptation was released in 1996, retitled *The Birdcage* and starring Nathan Lane, Robin Williams, Gene Hackman, Calista Flockhart and Christine Baranski. This adaptation suffers with many of the flaws that 1990s mainstream portrayals of minorities do; old stereotypes about gay men, drag queens or minority ethnicities are dragged up and made to dance until they're tired. However, the film saves its sharpest knives for the straight Republican couple and *The Birdcage* is worth watching for Nathan Lane's satirical turn as a dragged-up conservative woman whose litany of awful opinions the Republican couple love.

Ta
78.
The Arts

Vito Russo's book *The Celluloid Closet*, and later documentary of the same name, explores queer lives in Hollywood, both on camera and behind it. The book is now considered a landmark work thanks to its extensive and intensive study of the subject matter. Hollywood is Hollywood, though, and this isn't a dry history book but witty and truthful. It opens the door on Hollywood history that many are unaware of, including how the 1930 Production Code imposed strict rules on Hollywood, censoring portrayals of relationships – married couples had to have separate beds – alcohol, drugs, complex morality and, of course, queer lives. Movies would try to wriggle round these rules by 'coding' characters through their appearance and mannerisms so the audience would know they were queer, although sadly this would often be a way of marking the character as a villain or 'other'. Sadly, Russo died before the documentary was released but it too is considered a classic, narrated by Lily Tomlin (who was one of the film's biggest advocates) and featuring big name stars from Old Hollywood and new, including Tom Hanks, Tony Curtis, Quentin Crisp and Gore Vidal. GLAAD now give the Vito Russo Award to openly queer people in the film business who fight homophobia.

The Celluloid Closet

1981 (book);
1995 (documentary)

Book and documentary

Dykes to Watch Out For

1983–2008

Comic strip

79.

Alison Bechdel's multi-panel comic strip *Dykes to Watch Out For* ran for decades, from 1983 to 2008. There are several volumes collecting the strips, or you can find the later years online, on her website. The strip follows a slowly growing cast of lesbian, gay, genderqueer and trans people as they fall in and out of love, wrestle with the changing socio-political landscape and try to discover who they really are. It's a warm, self-conscious study of queer families (including chosen families); a subject that doesn't often come under the spotlight, even in queer culture.

80.

Ta
The Arts

Paris is Burning

1990

Documentary

If you have any interest in queer culture at all, know that this is *the* film and these are *the* references. Jennie Livingston's 1990 documentary chronicled the lives of African-American and Latino queer drag artists on the ball scene of New York. The camera follows legends and up-and-comers alike as they compete in balls and discuss their lives; their successes, their slang and their struggles to thrive in a white-centric heteronormative society. Every minute is transcendent, from Dorian Corey explaining shade (she doesn't have to *say* that you're ugly because you *know* that you're ugly), to transwomen Brooke and Carmen Xtravaganza frolicking on the beach, to the two young boys standing outside a Harlem ball at 3 a.m., explaining that this community is their true family. So much of what is seen in the documentary has filtered through to mainstream media that watching it seems like playing a game of 'Oh, that's where that's from'. If you can finish any of these sentences then you need to watch this film: 'Category is…', 'It is a known fact that a lady…', 'Touch this skin…' Lord help you if you think Madonna invented vogueing; you need to strap in and discover the House of LaBeija, House of Xtravaganza, House of Ninja, House of Duprée and House of Corey.

Stone Butch Blues

1993

Novel

81.

Ta
The Arts

Stone Butch Blues is a 1993 novel written by Leslie Feinberg: a tale of growing up as a butch lesbian in America in the seventies. Feinberg has said that the novel is not autobiographical, stating that *Stone Butch Blues* 'is a work of fiction, written by an author who has lived the non-fiction'. The tale explores gender identity and the search for a community that is supportive of the gender non-conforming main character. It won the 1994 American Library Association Gay & Lesbian Book Award and popularised the term 'stone butch'. In fact, *Stone Butch Blues* and Feinberg's subsequent non-fiction book *Transgender Warriors* helped establish the groundwork for much of the language centring around transgender issues. Feinberg was among the first people to use gender-neutral pronouns, preferring to be referred to as she or zie and her or hir. *Stone Butch Blues* is as much about the working class as it is about being queer and Feinberg campaigned as fiercely in hir lifetime for working class rights: a free PDF of *Blues* is available on hir website so everybody who wishes to can access it.

82.

Ta
The Arts

What do you get when you put three drag queens on an old bus (the eponymous Priscilla) and watch them drive through the Australian outback? Camp movie magic! Of course, the three queens, played by Hugo Weaving, Guy Pearce and Terence Stamp, exchange barbs and get embroiled in strange adventures, but the heart of the tale is one of love, family and realising one's self. The film knows perfectly well when to go gritty – as the queens encounter hostile locals in remote outback towns – glitzy – see Guy Pearce atop the bus, streaming a shimmering silver train – and sentimental – Terence Stamp's character, a transwoman, finding love in the unlikeliest of places. The film surpassed even the filmmaker's expectations, making millions worldwide and landing an Academy Award for costume design. It launched a well-received stage show that runs on both Broadway and in the West End, providing the audience with live-action drag thrills.

The Adventures of Priscilla, Queen of the Desert

1994 (movie);
2006 (musical)

Movie and musical

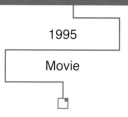

To Wong Foo, Thanks For Everything! Julie Newmar

1995

Movie

83.

Ta
The Arts

To Wong Foo isn't a perfect film but it is a big-name film made by a big-name studio, centred around three happy, healthy drag queens, which isn't easy to come by. Sure, the queens are played by three straight actors (if the film were released today, this casting decision may have caused some upset, as Hollywood continues to shun many queer actors, but Wesley Snipes absolutely owns his role as Noxeema Jackson) and yes, there is more than a touch of the sassy best friend trope abounding, but the film sparks with just enough wit and queer culture to make it worth a watch. The cameo list drips with drag prestige, with nearly every 1990s queer icon worth featuring, including RuPaul (as the excellently named Rachel Tensions), Joey Arias, Lady Bunny, Candis Cayne, Hedda Lettuce, Miss Coco Peru, and Quentin Crisp. Robin Williams, who helped to get the film made, also cameos, as does Miss Naomi Campbell herself.

Ta

84.

The Arts

Rent

The one-time longest-running show on Broadway, *Rent* is a riotous rock musical set during the time of the AIDS crisis in America. It follows a queer group of friends and lovers as they try to discover who they are and make enough money to at least pay the rent. The music is high-octane and the script is often witty, but the heart of the story comes from how the characters try to deal with the inescapable presence of HIV/AIDS in their lives. The original production and the film adaptation helped to launch the careers of musical superstar Idina Menzel and TV and film A-listers Rosario Dawson, Taye Diggs and Anthony Rapp.

1996 (musical); 2005 (movie)

Musical and movie

Hedwig and the Angry Inch

1998 (musical);
2001 (movie)

Musical and movie

85.

Ta
The Arts

Hedwig started life as an off-Broadway musical and grew into a queer film sensation. John Cameron Mitchell, who wrote and directed both the original musical and the film, originated one of the most iconic queer leading roles in film. Hedwig is the genderqueer lead singer of a rock band, styled in the androgynous glam rock tradition. She is wry, sharp and charismatic and holds the audience in the palm of her hand as she narrates and performs her journey from naïf in East Germany to 'internationally ignored' would-be rock star seeking justice from her plagiarising former lover. Although the film did not perform well financially on release, it became a cult classic and versions of the musical continued to run on Broadway. Famous actors who have taken up the wig on Broadway include Neil Patrick Harris, Michael C. Hall, Taye Diggs and Darren Criss.

86.

Ta
The Arts

Queer as Folk

The US adaption of Russell T. Davies' short series *Queer as Folk* means you can choose your own flavour when it comes to this tale of two gay twenty-somethings. Davies' original series was set in Manchester's famous Canal Street and ran for two series on Channel 4. If you would prefer your *Queer as Folk* short and sweet and are a sucker for a friends-to-lovers narrative, this is the one for you. If you like a longer running show to binge, with an extended cast of characters and a glossy American drama finish, then it sounds as though you should opt for the US adaptation. Both series were hits in their respective countries, although they garnered shock from some audience members with their frank discussions, and sometimes portrayals, of gay sex, drug use, pornography and homophobic attacks.

1999–2000 (UK);
2000–2005 (USA)

TV series

Moonlight

2016

Movie

Ta
The Arts

This coming-of-age tale took the prestigious Academy Award for Best Motion Picture (as well as Best Supporting Actor and Best Adapted Screenplay). Artistically shot, the film tells the story of people that are pushed to the margins in life and in the media. *Moonlight* consists of three acts, showing the main character Chiron as a boy, a teen and a young man. Lesser films could fall into the trap of showing only the miseries of a man who is young, black, poor, with an addict mother and who is questioning his own sexuality. The heart of *Moonlight* comes in the moments of real human connection, such as when he is befriended by his older neighbour, or the sweeping romanticism of his relationship with the boy, and then man, he longs for, Kevin.

Conclusion

Queer culture is not one defined thing but a great, shifting mass of astounding creation, as varied as humanity itself. It can be experienced in our clubs and on our streets but also on our bookshelves and through our speakers. Queer culture is a glossy blockbuster, a punk zine, a city-wide party and a work of art. It reflects us in all our flawed, funny, messy, sensible, brilliant glory. It's the conduit in which we can explore our identities and really see ourselves writ large and loud.

The list of luminaries, events and works in this book is by no means exhaustive. This is just a jumping-off point, a series of cultural highlights that will hopefully encourage you to follow the winding paths to the queer culture that most interests you. You may even thoroughly disagree with every selection in this book: if that is the case, I hope that you are inspired to create your own lists and share them, promoting the people that you love and the art that inspires you.

Support queer culture and help it grow. One of the best ways to do this is to support your local queer creators and attend the queer events that are happening in your area.

Finally, take a look at the end of this book for more; more charities to support, and more art that had to be mentioned.

More, More, More

Charities and Support Groups

The Terrence Higgins Trust
www.tht.org.uk

The Trevor Project
www.thetrevorproject.org

Stonewall
www.stonewall.org.uk

MindOut
www.mindout.org.uk

Mermaids
www.mermaidsuk.org.uk

Films

Mädchen in Uniform
Leontine Sagan

Un Chant D'Amour
Jean Genet

Pink Narcissus
James Bidgood

Querelle
Rainer Werner Fassbender

My Beautiful Launderette
Stephen Frears

Edward II
Derek Jarman

No Skin Off My Ass
Bruce LaBruce

Fucking Åmål
Lukas Moodyson

But I'm a Cheerleader
Jamie Babbit

Tangerine
Sean Baker

Carol
Todd Haynes

Queerarma
Daisy Asquith

Music

'Das Lila Lied' (The Lavender Song)
Kurt Schwabach and Mischa Spoliansky

Here's Little Richard
Little Richard

Rising Free
Tom Robinson Band

Klaus Nomi
Klaus Nomi

Indigo Girls
Indigo Girls

Imperfectly
Ani DiFranco

Ingénue
K. D Lang

Deflowered
Pansy Division

Stoosh
Skunk Anansie

69 Love Songs
The Magnetic Fields

Le Tigre
Le Tigre

Fatherfucker
Peaches

The Con
Tegan and Sara

Actor
St Vincent

Channel Orange
Frank Ocean

Too Bright
Perfume Genius

Transgender Dysmorphia Blues
Against Me!

Blue Neighbourhood
Troye Sivan

Literature

The Immoralist
André Gide

Death in Venice
Thomas Mann

Nightwood
Djuna Barnes

Confessions of a Mask
Yukio Mishima

Olive
Dorothy Bussy

The Price of Salt
Patricia Highsmith

Giovanni's Room
James Baldwin

The Persian Boy
Mary Renault

The Front Runner
Patricia Nell Warren

Tales of the City
Armistead Maupin

The Color Purple
Alice Walker

A Boy's Own Story
Edmund White

Annie On My Mind
Nancy Garden

Queer
William S. Burroughs

Gender Outlaw
Kate Bornstein

The Line of Beauty
Alan Hollinghurst

History

Coming Out
Jeffrey Weeks

And the Band Played On
Randy Shilts

Before Night Falls
Reinaldo Arenas

Transgender Warriors
Leslie Fienberg

*Sapphistries: A Global History of
Love Between Women*
Leila J. Rupp

Beyond Shame
Patrick Moore

*Bisexuality and the Eroticism of
Everyday Life*
Marjorie Garber

The Riddle of Gender
Deborah Rudacille

Transgender History
Susan Stryker

A Queer History of the United States
Michael Bronski

Queer: A Graphic History
Meg-John Barker

*David Bowie Made Me Gay:
100 Years of LGBT Music*
Darryl W Bullock

Queer City
Peter Ackroyd

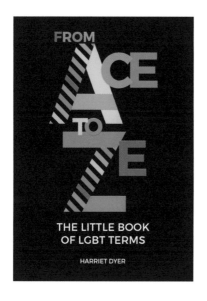

THE LITTLE BOOK
OF LGBT TERMS

HARRIET DYER

From Ace to Ze

Harriet Dyer

£6.99

978-1-78685-284-7

Paperback

Language is one of the key paths to awareness, acceptance and empowerment, but, honestly, it can be confusing for many people. This easy-to-use dictionary introduces some of the most essential terminology surrounding gender, sexuality and LGBTQ+ identity. If you have questions about yourself or about the terminology, or even if you're simply interested in learning more, this essential guide will help you navigate the world with knowledge and kindness.

If you're interested in finding out more
about our books, find us on Facebook
at Summersdale Publishers and follow
us on Twitter at @Summersdale.

www.summersdale.com